God of the Impossible

Rene O. Lopez

WESTBOW
PRESS®
A DIVISION OF THOMAS NELSON
& ZONDERVAN

WestBow Press books may be ordered through booksellers or by contacting:

WestBow Press
A Division of Thomas Nelson & Zondervan
1663 Liberty Drive
Bloomington, IN 47403
www.westbowpress.com
1 (866) 928-1240

Because of the dynamic nature of the Internet, any web addresses or links contained in this book may have changed since publication and may no longer be valid. The views expressed in this work are solely those of the author and do not necessarily reflect the views of the publisher, and the publisher hereby disclaims any responsibility for them.

Any people depicted in stock imagery provided by Getty Images are models, and such images are being used for illustrative purposes only.
Certain stock imagery © Getty Images.

Scripture quotations marked (NLT) are taken from the Holy Bible, New Living Translation, copyright ©1996, 2004, 2015 by Tyndale House Foundation. Used by permission of Tyndale House Publishers, Inc., Carol Stream, Illinois 60188. All rights reserved.

Scripture taken from the New King James Version®. Copyright © 1982 by Thomas Nelson. Used by permission. All rights reserved.

Scripture quotations marked (NIV) are taken from the Holy Bible, New International Version®, NIV®. Copyright © 1973, 1978, 1984, 2011 by Biblica, Inc.™ Used by permission of Zondervan. All rights reserved worldwide. www. zondervan.com The "NIV" and "New International Version" are trademarks registered in the United States Patent and Trademark Office by Biblica, Inc.™

ISBN: 978-1-9736-7229-6 (sc)
ISBN: 978-1-9736-7228-9 (hc)
ISBN: 978-1-9736-7230-2 (e)

Library of Congress Control Number: 2019912661

Printed in the United States of America.

WestBow Press rev. date: 02/03/2020

This book is dedicated to Rosa Lopez

Contents

Introduction

When my family and I first arrived in Toronto, Canada, on May 31, 1983 after leaving El Salvador, my country of birth, I had a dream. My dream did not originate in Toronto, but it originated in a city called Orange Walk, Belize. It was there that I attended a movie theater for the first time. My heart was filled with emotions as I watched the world's greatest Agent 007 combat his greatest enemies. My imagination also soared as I watched Bruce Lee fight off every one of his opponents.

Every weekend you would find me at the local racetrack in Orange Walk, Belize. At the age of eight, my first work was to find all the empty beer bottles on the grounds of the track and bring them back to the vendor, where I would be paid a certain amount for one bottle. (I think I was paid one penny for a bottle). Once I had made enough money for the day, I would sprint across the city and try to catch the next 007 or Bruce Lee movie.

As I sat at the theater and watch my heroes do what they did best, I remember whispering to myself, "One day I want to be up there. I want to be like James Bond or Bruce Lee."

When we arrived in Canada, keeping my dream alive was easy. In those days, Toronto was considered to be the "second Hollywood". At the age of ten, I attended acting classes. When classes were over, I hired my first agent. My dreams were being fulfilled.

While life seemed good on the surface, things at home were not so favorable. Mom and Dad constantly quarreled with each other. Mom was a clerk at a store while dad worked in construction. Dad was a gifted man. His melodious voice and skills at composing songs were both a blessing and a curse. My father had a very short fuse and would get angry for the smallest detail. Although my family was not perfect, the God of the impossible was at work in us and would do something amazing through us.

My parents separated when I was fourteen years of age. This was the best news we could have received, especially for our mother, who for years had experienced many trials. A couple of months before Mom and dad separated, I remember getting into an intense argument with Dad. Once he figured out that he could not win his arguments with me, I was told to leave the house, and that is exactly what I did. Since I was still in school, I needed to survive, so I began breaking into people's cars at different parking lots. I use the phrase break in very loosely as I actually did not break anything. My mode of operation was to find any car that was left unlocked, and when I could not find any, I would look for their emergency key that would be stuck to a magnet under the car. I did this because hunger and fatigue were my best friends, and I was in need of food and stability in my life. Therefore, I got a job...at a parking lot.

By the time I was sixteen, my dreams took me to San Francisco, where I would have an encounter with the God of the impossible. It was there that I gave my life and dreams to the God of the impossible. One morning I whispered to God these words, "Lord, take my dreams. Take my life. I am Yours. Let Your will be done in my life and not my will. Guide me every day of my life."

After I gave my heart to Jesus and experienced this overwhelming joy, I knew that I had to forgive my dad just as Christ had forgiven me, so I began to pray that my father would have an encounter with Jesus. After sixteen years of lifting my father up to the Lord in prayer, I had an unexpected phone call from my dad. He reached out to me while we were living in Virginia.

His words were unforgettable. "Son, what are you doing this week-end?" he asked.

"I am busy at church, dad. Why? What is the matter?" I asked him with bewilderment.

"I just thought that you could come down to Toronto for the week-end and baptize me."

My heart was overjoyed as I heard my Dad say that his heart belonged to Jesus and he wanted me to confirm his decision through baptism. I am proud to share with you that on October 26, 2002, I had the privilege of baptizing my father. The God of the impossible had done the impossible by answering one of my prayers, and yet God is not done with my life. The God of the impossible has something wonderful for you. Ask Him to be your King and your Guide. Trust that the God of the impossible will do the impossible in your life.

The night my father was dying, I stood by his bed side and asked him some important questions. These questions were not asked for his sake, but for all who were present. I said, "Dad, can you hear me?" He looked straight at me and nodded his head in affirmation. "I want to ask you some questions and just nod if you agree." My father was frail, yet he managed to stare straight at me and answered positively to every one of these questions.

Dad, do you still love Jesus? Do you accept Jesus as your Lord and King? Do you accept the sacrifice He made on your behalf by dying on the cross and offering you eternal salvation? Do you accept the forgiveness he offers for your sins? Do you still believe that one day soon, our Lord will come back for us and take us home?

After he answered all these questions, I grabbed Dad's hands and said, "I will see you when Jesus comes."

That was the last I saw him alive. I love my father, and I know that one day when Jesus comes back for us, I will see my dad once more. This time around, we will never say goodbye again.

My child hood dreams are not dead yet. I still dream of one day appearing in a Christian movie, even though I have not seen a movie set since the spring of 1989. For now, I am grateful for the journey my God, the God of the impossibilities has led me through. He has brought us to Hawaii (tough job, but somebody has to do it). It is here that I have the privilege of ministering to a beautiful church we call ohana (family).

Each chapter of this book is filled with experiences from Bible characters and from my own life journey. I pray that you will have as much fun reading this book as I had writing it.

Remember, the God of the impossible wants to do the impossible possible in your life.

Acknowledgments

Everything I have accomplished I owe it to my God. He makes me smile day in and day out. His plans for me are bigger than what I can imagine.

Thank you is not enough for what my mother has taught me through her example and faith in the God of the impossible.

My wife Jessika, and my three girls, Jessika, Celina and Daniella are an inspiration to me. Your love for God and for the ministry is why I love doing what I do. May God bless you in all you do. I can't wait to see what the God of the impossible has for your lives. I love you.

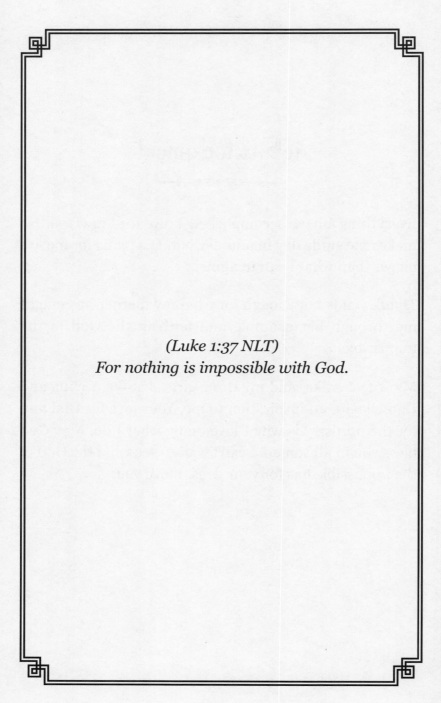

(Luke 1:37 NLT)
For nothing is impossible with God.

God of the Impossible

It was one of those memorable days when school was out early. Children were dashing home from school, and college students were just getting warmed up for their expected Friday soccer game. There was nothing out of the ordinary. It was just what you would anticipate on a bright, fair day in Costa Rica. Jessika and I were just months into our new school known as marriage. We had committed ourselves to each other and promised to love one another until death separates us. Every Friday afternoon, we would stroll away from college campus and head to the market place, where we would indulge ourselves with the best produce Costa Rica had to offer. On this particular afternoon, we decided to skip our usual walk from campus and instead we chose to wait for the bus to appear.

Our campus was distinctive from other campuses within the country, for it housed a number of students ranging from elementary school to college. Most of the college students were from all over North and Central America. This made it a unique setting that would teach us about our unsurpassed Creator.

1

My heart was pleased to see the little children heading home. Some children were juggling their soccer balls, and others were hustling, as if engaged in a speeding contest. Others seemed complacent to get home without a rush. In front of the college campus was a road that went from the city of Alajuela to one of nature's spectacular volcanos known as Poas. This narrow, winding road barely had room for two vehicles, making it a very dangerous path for all- especially for the school children. Unwary motorists would speed by the campus, as if they were oblivious to the school children surrounding them.

As we were standing at the bus stop anticipating our ride, I took a quick glance to my right, the direction we were headed for. Then I turned to my left to see if the bus was coming. Children were running from one direction to the other. One more time, I scanned to my right, and then to my left. In the distance was a black pickup truck descending the hill and gaining momentum. Children were crossing the street without a care. I quickly observed to my right and then my left. I noticed the black truck was speeding down the hill without slowing down. After another quick look at my right, suddenly I heard a screech, followed by my wife's scream and finally a loud bang. As I turned to my left, I saw a young girl twisting up in the air, as if in slow motion. She came down and hit the asphalt violently. The driver's failed attempt at avoiding the child caused him to swerve to his right, missing a couple of more children by inches. His truck came to a stop as he crashed into the campus wall.

Without hesitation, I ran to the child's aid. Chaos reigned as her brothers were terrified, standing beside their lifeless sister.

Passing by the main gate of the campus, I screamed to the gate keeper, "Call for an ambulance!".

Her two older brothers were in shock and in fear of losing their sibling. One of them was screaming and crying, blaming himself for what had just transpired. "My mother!" he yelled. "My mother will kill me for not being a good brother! I did not take good care of my sister!"

Crowds gathered around the campus wall. Some were silent and in shock and others hollered for nurses to come and help. When I finally reached the child, I could see blood coming from her mouth. Her body was motionless. Time was at a standstill. I grabbed her hand and reached for the hand of one of her brothers. I asked him if he believed that with God all things are possible?

He nodded while I screamed, "Let's pray!"

A wave of emotions came over me as we continued pouring our hearts out to God, with nurses from the university rushing in. A siren was wailing in the distance. The ambulance was on its way. It normally took a very long time for the ambulance to arrive. This was indeed a miracle in itself. The ambulance was there in less than fifteen minutes.

The driver of the pickup was drunk and confused. His demeanor showed remorse for the mess he had created.

As my wife and I were seated at Friday night's vespers, I could not shake off the images of the day's event. Suddenly, our pastor came to the podium with a special announcement regarding the child. As he started speaking, his voice quivered, his eyes watered, and then a big smile suddenly appeared.

"The child will live," he announced. "She suffered nothing more than broken front teeth."

Everyone in the audience broke out with great "Amen". Truly we serve the God of the impossible.

Impossible Made Possible

Journey with me back in time to a place where the God of the impossible would alter the life of another young girl. This story takes us to the hills of lower Galilee some thirteen hundred feet above sea level, to a town known as Nazareth. A young lady by the name of Mary received an unusual visit from an unusual guest. God sent his angel Gabriel to deliver amazing news to Mary. It was just not any news; this was the mother of all news. Mary was the fortunate one. She had been chosen to be the mother of the Messiah, Jesus, the Savior of the world.

> *Mary was frightened at the sight of the angel, but the angel said, "Do not be afraid, Mary, for you have found favor with God."*
> *(Luke 1:30 NLT)*

After hearing the angel's words, Mary was confused. The news must have hit her like a tabloid headline. She must have wondered why the angel insisted on calling her "greatly favored". Feeling a bit distressed by all that was happening before her, she probably had some questions she felt necessary to ask her guest. Everything that the angel said to her, came as a shock, a surprise, and it would have mystified the best of us. When she finally realized what was actually happening, she must have wondered, "Are you sure you got the right address? Is your GPS working properly? You do know that I am a virgin, right?"

I don't think it was every young lady's dream to be the mother of the Messiah. Sure, they must have all heard from the religious teachers that sooner or later God would provide them with a liberator. However, since much time had passed from the first mention of the Savior's coming, most likely many were not even looking for him. News about a Savior was written all over the Torah, including how the Messiah would come from David's ancestry.

The angel Gabriel brought Mary news of great proportions. He spoke these words as he turned to Mary and said, "You, Mary, will become pregnant and you shall call your child Jesus."

Mary probably exclaimed to the angel, "That is great news indeed, but, hello? Have you not heard? Do you not realize that although I am engaged, I have not gotten married? This is the reason why I am almost certain that you must surely have the wrong person. Joseph and I have not slept together yet, so you must have mistaken my identity. Maybe your GPS has misled you to the wrong house. Or maybe you read your texts and emails wrong. I am sure that you are aware of my marriage status. You should have checked my Facebook profile before coming here. You see,

Gabriel, since I am not married and have not had sex, it is impossible for me to have a child."

Little did Mary realize that her cousin, who had been unable to have children was now into her sixth month. Yes, Elizabeth, Mary's cousin, could not have a baby. Elizabeth and her husband had tried and tried again but without success. Finally, they gave up hope of ever having a child. People called Elizabeth "the barren one."[1] That was her nick name. To be barren in those days was not a good thing. Rumors had it that if a woman was barren it was because God was surely punishing her for her sins. They had no fertility centers in those days, but they did have something that you and I have access to: prayer. Our God loves to answer the call of His children, and there is nothing too difficult for Him. He is the God of the impossible.

Always remember what Luke 1:37 (NKJV) says: *"For with God nothing will be impossible."* It does not matter what situation you are facing in life. No matter how difficult it may seem, God will make a way for you. There is nothing too difficult for Him. Look in the mirror, and realize that you are very valuable in God's sight. You have been brought to this little planet called earth for a reason. God has a great future for you, so do not throw in the towel. Instead, drop to your knees and realize that there is no other God like our God.

---

[1] Luke 1:36 (NLT)

In the Bible is a text that I love to read, because it reinforces just what I am telling you. You are here for a purpose. You are not an accident. As a matter of fact, in God's sight, you are the most beautiful person on this planet. You are worth more than life itself. Here is what God wrote to you in His love letter, which is also known as the Bible: "'For I know the plans I have for you,' says the LORD. 'They are plans for good and not for disaster, to give you a future and a hope'" (Jeremiah 29:11 NLT).

Did you catch that? God brought you here for a reason; He has a plan for you and your loved ones. It was never in His plans for you to go through life with uncertainties. You may not know what tomorrow will bring, but that is okay because He knows. He has the whole world in His hands. He knows where you live, and He knows what worries you. He knows every little minute details of your life. He laughs when you laugh, He cries when you cry, and He holds you in the palm of His hands.

> "See, I have written your name on my hand."
> (Isaiah 49:16 NLT)

Although Mary did not understand the whole picture, she was moved to accept God's plans for her. She humbled herself and replied:

> *"I am the Lord's servant, and I am willing to accept whatever he wants. May everything you have said come true..." (Luke 1:38 NLT)*

At that time the angel left her, yet she was never alone. God was with her just as He had been before Mary received the news. God is with you as well. He has never abandoned you, nor will He do it now.

His Battle

There is yet another story I want to share with you, and it is found in Exodus 14. God's people were slaves in Egypt for over four hundred years and now it was time for the Israelites to be delivered. With an awesome display of His power, God set His people free.

God made a promise to Abraham, and it also applies to all of us. This promise is found in Genesis 12:3. It basically says that we belong to God, we are not alone in this world, and however someone treats us, that is how God will treat them.

> *"I will bless those who bless you and curse those who curse you." (Genesis 12:3 NLT)*

The nation of Israel was God's chosen people, just like you are His chosen child. Our Creator has created you for a reason, for a purpose. You are not a mistake. You were wonderfully made. God's thoughts towards you are overwhelming. He believes in you. He believes in your dreams, and He wants nothing more than to see you accomplish all your goals and aspirations. The Bible says, "How precious are your thoughts about me, O God! They are innumerable!" (Psalm 139:17).

Back to the story...God had given strict orders to Moses, Israel's leader. God's people were to set camp between a "rock and a hard place," so to speak. The Israelites were instructed by God Himself to camp beside the sea, where they could be easy prey for Pharaoh and his army. God's plan would be considered foolish by any human standard. To camp beside the sea without any escape route is... reckless! Wait! God has a plan. He always has a plan. He had a plan for the Israelites. He has a plan for you, and His strategy will never fail.

As the Egyptian army rushed closer to their prey, people began to panic and cried to God for help. It seemed that God was not listening to their cries.

They rushed to Moses, saying, "Weren't there enough graves in Egypt? Why did you bring us here to this wilderness to die?" (Exodus 14:11 NLT)

Undisturbed by all the commotion, Moses reassured them that God had a plan for them. God will never abandon His children. He will never abandon you. Moses looked at them and pronounced these words:

> *"The LORD himself will fight for you. You won't have to lift a finger in your defense!" (Exodus 14:14 NLT)*

What Moses was saying is that this battle is not yours. Let God take care of it for you. Whatever you are dealing with, take it to God and let Him handle it. There is nothing too hard for the Lord. Nothing is impossible for our God. Nothing is beyond His reach.

That cancer you are dealing with? Take it to God. Problems at home? Take them to God. You are not sure how you will pay next month's rent? He does. Take it to God. I once read this quote on Facebook:

"When the storms of life drop you to your knees...stay there and pray."

The Israelites were afraid, as they should have been. They were trapped, with nowhere to run, nowhere to hide. Behind them were Pharoah's top soldiers with their commanders, six hundred chariots in all.

Have you ever felt that way? That you are stuck in between a rock and a hard place? Have you felt that you had nowhere to go? God told them to move forward. God tells Moses to lift up his rod and the sea would be divided. God's children were to move forward in faith.

As the Israelites moved forward, God did the impossible again. He divided the sea and made the ground dry so that His children would pass through the sea on dry ground.

> *"So the people of Israel walked through the sea on dry ground, with walls of water on each side!" (Exodus 14:22 NLT)*

How cool is that! As God's children moved forward on dry ground, to their sides they were protected by walls of water. You know what I would have done if I was there and I saw to my right and to my left a wall of water? I would have stopped and plunged my face through that wall, and while I was at it, maybe I would even try to catch a fish or two with my teeth.

God made the impossible possible back then and God can make the impossible possible now. You might ask yourself, "How can God do the impossible in my life? My student loan is mounting up. My medical bills are increasing. I don't know how to help my kids. I can't seem to find a job."

As I was writing down some thoughts on paper, my cell phone rang. I did not recognize the number on the screen. When I answered the phone, a soft voice asked to speak to Pastor Lopez. After I identified myself, she said, "My brother was a believer. Now he is slowly dying away at your local hospital. All the family is flying there to meet with him one last time. Pastor, are you able to visit him at the hospital?" After our conversation I went on my knees and asked God to help and guide our visit with this gentleman I have never met before. I was at the hospital about forty-five minutes after my conversation with the patient's sister. When I reached his room and went inside, I whispered to God, "Do the impossible for him." Inside the room was a very thin, ailing, pale man. After I spent time with him, it became evident why his family was willing to make the long trip just to be with him one more time. The doctors did not give him a favorable prognosis.

After praying for him, I asked if he would allow me to come back the next day with some of my church elders with the intention of anointing him with oil and lifting him up in prayer. Before I left the room, I encouraged him to talk to God that night and acknowledge his sins to our Heavenly Father. He agreed. The next day, two of my elders and I came to his bedside and performed an anointing ceremony, followed by much prayer.

Four days later, his sister called me once more. This time her spirit was one of joy and praise. "Pastor," she said, "thank you for anointing my brother. Most of the family is in town and wanted to surprise him with our visit. However, we are the ones surprised at the news we received today as we came to his side. The doctors have cleared him to go home tomorrow. Our brother will be fine. Thank you, Pastor."

Put your trust in an all-knowing, all-powerful God. You may not know the future, but He does. He sees beyond what we see.

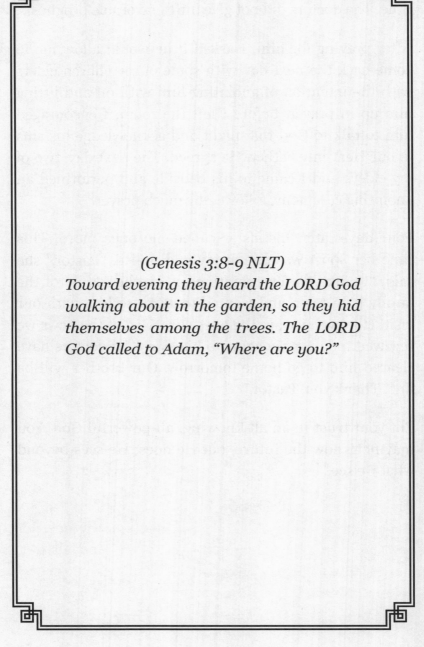

(Genesis 3:8-9 NLT)
Toward evening they heard the LORD God walking about in the garden, so they hid themselves among the trees. The LORD God called to Adam, "Where are you?"

Where Are You?

We were heading to my grandmother's house when our pickup truck stopped to let another passenger in. Since the back of the truck was already crowded enough with as many family members we could fit in, one more rider would not do us any harm.

My uncle was the nominated driver, and because most of us grew up in North America, we wanted to feel and experience what it was like to ride in the back of a truck. Since the family was big in numbers, I was not familiar with all the names of each passenger. I especially did not know this young man that we had just picked up. His appearance was one that demanded respect. His eyes displayed his life struggles, and a lack of serenity was present.

My eyes tried hard not to stare at him or at all his tattoos. Each tattoo displayed the details about which gang his loyalty belonged to. Although his scars attempted to hide his age, his face showed a disparity, and one could only assume his age at fourteen or fifteen.

Riding in the back of the truck with a very young gangster made me become aware of how fortunate my life had been. Growing up in Toronto was nothing compared to what this teenager had been facing all his young life.

As we ventured to my grandmother's house, I kept hearing a voice in my mind instructing me to "tell him about Me." Again, the voice reverberated louder, "Tell him about Me." I knew it was God asking. No! God was commanding me to tell this young man that God had called him to a better life, a life with a purpose and an aim.

I felt that Jesus wanted me to introduce this young gangster to his Savior, his King, "But how could I do that?" I kept telling myself. "He is a gang member. He has lived a life full of violence, and the last thing he wants is for me to tell him about Jesus. No. I cannot. Not now. Tomorrow! I will tell him about You, Lord, tomorrow."

For the next fifty minutes, I kept fighting with this voice in my mind directing me to tell this young man about Jesus. My will was overpowering the will of God. "Tomorrow Lord, I will tell him tomorrow. Besides, he doesn't even know me. He is going to laugh and think that I am just another weird "Jesus freak."

We arrived at Grandmother's home, and everyone got out of the truck and entered her home, with the exception of this young man. "Are you coming in?" I asked. "I got stuff to do, I'll see you guys tomorrow," he shouted back as he was making his way to the main intersection.

The following day the phone rang, and my grandmother answered. From my room I could hear Grandma say, "Just a minute."

A few seconds later, she hollered my name out. I ran towards her as she pointed to the phone. I slowly grabbed the phone and said, "Hola."

"Rene, don't ask any questions. Just listen to my instructions and follow them carefully. I will explain when you get here. Please grab the truck and go to the nearest funeral home. Buy the cheapest coffin you can find, and then come to the morgue. We will be here waiting for you."

The voice on the other side sounded somewhat faint, and indistinct. I followed the orders without saying a word. When I arrived at the city morgue, I found a number of people scattered around a metal bed. On this bed was a body covered with white sheets. A sense of fear crept over me, as I got close to the metal table. I was curious and wanted to find out who was under the sheets. I slowly pulled away the covers, unveiling his face. I could not believe who I was seeing. My emotions came crashing at me like a runaway eighteen-wheeler. I could not speak, my body felt numb, and I felt like I was about to throw up. I ran outside to get some air. I was in utter shock. I bent over, holding my stomach, when I heard the voice again: "Why didn't you tell him about Me?" I was very emotional at the thought that I had disobeyed my Master's voice and now this young man was dead, with two bullet holes in his face.

I remember how I kept telling God, "Tomorrow, Lord, I will tell him tomorrow." Tomorrow never came for this young man. God was calling me to tell him about this wonderful God we serve. The call was urgent, and I had failed Him miserably.

From that moment on, I promised my Lord that wherever He would take me, I would not remain silent. Our God loves us so much. All He wants is for us to give Him our hearts, and in turn He will give us the gift of eternal life found only in Jesus.

In my life I have given my Lord many reasons why He should not love me. None of these reasons are valid for Him. He is in the business of looking for the lost. He loves you with a love that cannot be understood or explained. Give your heart to Jesus now, before it is too late. Our lives are not in our hands. Only God knows the future. Trust Jesus with your whole life, your heart, your worries, your concerns. Surrender to Jesus now. Give Him your all.

The Garden of Eden

The moment God placed Adam and Eve in the garden, he gave the pair instructions as to what they were and were not able to eat. God said to them: "You may freely eat the fruit of every tree in the garden except the tree of the knowledge of good and evil. If you eat its fruit, you are sure to die" (Genesis 2:16-17 NLT).

The instructions seemed simple enough, right? They were able to eat of any tree except one. The mango, the pineapple, the watermelon, the papaya, and all other wonderful fruits were a go, except one. We are not told what type of fruit the tree produced, but the commandment was simple enough. I believe that God's instructions to Eve went something like this: "Do not eat it, no matter how good it may look, no matter how good it may feel. Do not eat from that tree." What would happen should they disobey the command? "You are sure to die." (Genesis 2:17 NLT)

We are not told how much time elapsed since the command was given. We do know that Eve somehow was engaged in a conversation with an animal. Eve was talking with an animal, and not just any animal. No, it was not the donkey. That was another story. The Bible tells us that Eve was conversing with a serpent. Yes, you heard correctly, a serpent (una serpiente).

The Bible describes the serpent as being more cunning than any animal ever created. Two words come to mind when I think of the word cunning: *artfulness* and *trickery*. Let us imagine all that transpired that day.

Eve is walking in the garden when suddenly she hears a voice coming from one of the trees. The voice is soft, lovely to the ears, very interesting and not to mention, flattering. Picture this serpent calling Eve by saying, "Eve, you look breathtaking. God indeed saved the best for last. Not only do you look great, but you smell great. Come closer, Eve. I want to admire your beauty."

By this time Eve was flabbergasted. No one except her husband had ever spoken to her in that manner. She knew it was not God, for she knew Gods' voice. Could it be some angel? As she pondered about the identity of the voice she moved slowly toward the forbidden tree.

For Adam and Eve, life in the garden was perfect. The air was pure, and the days were never hot or never cold. Although they walked around without any covers on, they did not realize their nakedness. Their innocence was like that of a child. Children run around naked without a care in the world. They play with their friends not worrying about the color or race of the other child. That is how Adam and Eve were at first. Innocent. As long as they remained true to their Creator and followed His command, all remain the same.

Once she was at the forbidden tree, she heard the voice once more, and it was asking, "Did God really say you must not eat the fruit from any of the trees in the garden?" (Genesis 3:1 NLT) Wait a minute…stop the press. This serpent is being crafty with his words. This serpent was trying to put doubt in Eve's mind regarding God and His credibility. The serpent was lying about God. When Jesus spoke to the religious leaders of his day this is what he had to say regarding the devil, "… He has always hated the truth, because there is no truth in him. When he lies, it is consistent with his character; for he is a liar and the father of lies" (John 8:44 NLT).

While listening to this creature, Eve was looking all around this tree trying to find the mysterious creature, and then she spotted it. It was beautiful. She had seen many serpents in the garden before, but none had ever spoken to her.

You see, every time the devil appears to us, it is to trick us. He does not appear as a horrible monster with horns, and a tail and holding a fork in his hands. No. When the enemy appears to us, he comes in a beautiful, innocent fashion. He comes to us with a clear mission in mind: to destroy all that is dear to you. Even worse, the enemy comes to destroy your faith in God. The deceiver has had many years to study you and to know your weakness. He may tempt you to lust after a beautiful woman, awakening your desire for her, resulting in the destruction of your marriage. Your children suffer the most when you give in to the enemy's craftiness. Maybe the enemy does not appear to you in that manner. He may appear to you in the form of alcohol, drugs, money or fame. It does not matter how the deceiver appears to you. His goal is to keep you as far away from God as possible. It is the enemy's goal to keep us from trusting the God of the impossible. He wants to destroy our marriages, our lives, and even the lives of our loved ones. When we give in to temptation, there are always consequences of insurmountable heights.

Eve knew the answer to that question. What the serpent said was not true. Eve therefore answered, "Of course we may eat fruit from the trees in the garden. It's only the fruit from the tree in the middle of the garden that we are not allowed to eat. God said, 'You must not eat it or even touch it; if you do, you will die'" (Genesis 3:3 NLT)

Eve was right on the money. She knew exactly what her Creator had instructed. She even went further by letting the serpent know that not only eating the fruit brought consequences but touching it as well.

As we ponder the events unfolding before us, have you asked yourself one important question: Why is Eve dialoguing with an animal? You see, nowhere in the Bible do we find that God gave animals the ability of reason. Yes, I agree animals are smart, cute, and furry (especially dogs), but they were not endowed with the capabilities that we possess. As I sit in front of my computer, my dog (Rocky) is lying beside my feet. What would happen if Rocky tugged at my pant and yelled at me, "Hey, buddy, will you feed me already?" I do not know what you would do if your cat started talking to you. However, I would run out of my house in a heartbeat.

I understand that there are psychics who claim they can talk to animals, specially the dead ones. That is crazy. Claiming to be able to speak with dead animals is truly ludicrous. The enemy is working full time and overtime in order to trick us. Do not believe these people who claim they have been gifted and are able to communicate with the beasts, especially, dead ones.

When Eve spoke to the serpent, she did not realize that it was the enemy using the serpent as a medium to communicate lies to Eve and her partner. If the enemy was able to entice the angels in heaven, then know that we are not exempt from his hypnotic powers. God probably sent warnings to Adam and his wife regarding the great battle between good and evil. I can only imagine that the couple was warned by the angels and by God Himself. These heavenly messengers would come to the garden and spend time with Adam and Eve. The Bible tells us that God Himself walked around the garden. Adam and Eve enjoyed their encounter with God. They spoke to Him face-to-face. And I am happy to say that one day soon, you and I will speak to God face-to-face.

Second Lie

Before Eve could explain her answer, the serpent formulated yet another lie: "You won't die!" (Genesis 3:4 NLT).

Did you catch that? Another lie! The serpent was misleading Eve into doubting God and His words. When God speaks, He cannot lie (Hebrews 6:18). It is impossible for our King, our Creator to lie. When He says that He will never abandon you, He means He will never abandon you. He cannot lie! When He told Eve that if she ate of the forbidden fruit she would die, that's exactly what He meant.

The father of lies, Satan, always wraps his words with ambiguity. His duplicity enshrouds us with a sense of mystery, doubt and curiosity.

I recall hearing how someone had a drinking problem. This person started drinking at a very early age. It was at a social party that he began drinking. Everything started innocently until his drinking enslaved him to the point of death. Having lost most of his savings to addictions, he came home one day with the stench of alcohol on his body. He went to his room looking for his weapon. After successfully finding his gun, he went to the living room, where his wife and children were watching television. As he muttered his last words, he took his life, having no consideration for his family.

The enemy uttered his deceitful words to Eve: "God knows that your eyes will be opened as soon as you eat it, and you will be like God" (Genesis 3:5 NLT).

Although God wants us to be like Him in character, He wants us to love like He loves, to forgive as He has forgiven, and to show mercy and compassion to those around us. We can never be like God, simply because there is only one God, one Creator, one Savior. He is Creator. We are His creation.

> *Have you never heard? Have you never understood? The LORD is the everlasting God, the Creator of all the earth. He never grows weak or weary. No one can measure the depths of his understanding. (Isaiah 40:28 NLT)*

By contradicting God's words to Eve. Satan, the father of all lies, challenged the veracity of God's words by concealing it with another lie, "You will be like God."[2] What Satan was eventually telling Eve was that God did not want another god around. Satan made it seem that God, our Creator was envious and did not want Adam and Eve to be truly happy. I can hear him say to Eve, "God does not want other rivals around. Right now, you don't have all the truth simply because your eyes are not wide open. However, when you eat of the forbidden fruit your eyes will be open."

Make no mistake about it-Satan's nature is one of blasphemy. His ultimate goal is to be like God. He wants to have his own throne and situate it next to God's throne. Therefore, by doing this, Satan thought to have equal sovereign power. Look up Isaiah 14:12-14.

Regrettably, the serpent managed to pique at Eve's curiosity. Eve saw that the fruit was good to eat and it was very desirable, able to make her wise. Maybe the serpent himself took one bite of the fruit, just to close the deal. "See, I am not dead, and I touched the fruit," is what the serpent probably said. Eve gave in to temptation and disobeyed God's words by eating the forbidden fruit.

A couple in Turmoil

One evening I felt compelled to visit one of our faithful church members at their home. "Pastor, I was praying to the Lord that He would bring you to my home. My neighbors are wonderful people. They have two children.

---

[2] New King James Version,

However, I suspect that they are heading for a divorce. Pastor, can you go to their home? Let them know that I sent you, and please pray for their marriage." This beautiful grandmother was one of my fervent prayer warriors, and when she spoke, I listened.

Before I headed to the neighbor's home, I bowed my head and prayed to the God of the impossible, "Lord, whatever is going on in the lives of these people, Your children, do the impossible possible for them."

There I was ringing the doorbell of someone I had never met. How would they react to a total stranger coming to their home to pray for them? I was not sure of the answers. I just knew that when God asks us to do something, we must do it. No matter how difficult or awkward the request may seem, when we are sure God is leading, we put faith into action.

The doorbell kept ringing over and over, until I felt like quitting. After what seemed like an eternity, the door opened. A tall, heavily built, athletic man looked at me and said, "May I help you?"

My knees were shaking. My palms were sweaty. My voice was quivery. I said, "Your neighbor asked me to come over and introduce myself to you. I am Pastor Lopez, and I am here to pray for you. Is there anything in particular that you feel I should pray for?"

This strong man did something that caught me off guard. He began to tear up and said, "My wife is off to see her lawyer. She wants a divorce. Please come in, Pastor. It's cold out there."

I slowly made my way to their living room and sat myself on their sofa. After making myself comfortable and allowing him time to catch his breath, I had the audacity to ask, "Why are you getting a divorce? How long have you been married?"

He responded by explaining, "After twenty years of marriage, our trust in each other has disappeared."

As he was explaining their distrust for each other, tears rolled down his face. They had been attending marriage counselling for months, to no avail. Their friends counseled them to divorce. Their parents counseled them to divorce. Not even their counselor could not find a reason they should stay married. Their case was almost impossible. Everyone had given up hope on their marriage.

When everyone has given up hope on you; when everyone has given up on your marriage, or when everyone says that there is nothing that can be done, look up. All is not as it seems. There is hope. Sit up and lift your hands to the God of the impossible. Get on your knees and spill your heart out to the only one who is able to help. His name is Jesus. Everyone may give up on you, except Jesus. He has not and will not give up on you and your family. Your marriage counselor says it is impossible for you to love one another again...but Jesus is love. Come to the fountain of hope, the fountain of wisdom. Come to Jesus. "For with God all things are possible." (Luke 1:37 NLT)

This man was a hero. After he had served our country for our freedom, I was not going to let him go without bringing his case to the ultimate Judge-the God of the impossible. We both fell to our knees. I placed my hand on this man's shoulder and prayed. Soon, we both were praying. I prayed for restoration while he prayed for forgiveness. As we both prayed our hearts out, we could sense that the God of the Impossibility was about to do something great.

Two weeks had gone by when I received a phone call requesting for me to come see this couple. When I had arrived, I was told that the wife did not file for divorce. As we were praying, two weeks ago, his wife was struck by a wave of good memories. She recalled how they had met. A recollection of their first date and their first kiss made her shed some tears. Memories of his proposing to her flooded her mind.

"I'll give us one more chance," she told herself as she stormed out of her lawyers' office. Suddenly hope had rekindled her love for him.

Just when we think it's over, God has the last word. He is the God of the impossible and wants to do the impossible in your life. Come to Him and place your life in His hands. Trust in His promises and wait for the impossible to be done.

(Genesis 3:6 NLT)
"The woman was convinced. She saw that the tree was beautiful and its fruit looked delicious, and she wanted the wisdom it would give her. So she took some of the fruit and ate it. Then she gave some to her husband, who was with her, and he ate it, too."

Where Are You? Part 2

The serpent had conquered Eve's mind which lead her to doubt God's goodness. She looked at the forbidden fruit with desire. She saw that it was appealing to the eyes. Just the thought of eating the fruit exhilarated her senses. Scripture tells us that she ate of the forbidden fruit and also gave some to her husband.

Adam and Eve were both naked in the garden. Their innocence had not allowed them to conceal what they didn't perceive. Like little children playing in their simplicity, so were our first parents. After they had their first bite of the forbidden fruit and had disobeyed God, some part of their innocence had vanished away. They saw their vulnerability. They felt cold and scared. At that same moment, they saw a leaf fall from a tree. Their environment had been forever altered.

Before they took that fateful bite of the forbidden fruit, they felt safe and secure. After their fall, a sense of fear fell upon them, permeating their very surroundings. Realizing their nakedness, brought only shame and guilt upon the pair. Suddenly an idea dawned upon them. What if they sewed together some leaves to cover their exposed skin?

If only the couple had listened to God's command and not let curiosity prevail. Surely, they would have evaded feeling miserable. If they would have listened to God's counsel, they would not have gotten hurt.

We may feel a sense of excitement when we are with someone who seems to care enough to listen. When our spouses are too busy to even notice us, it's easy to be swept away by a forbidden fruit. This forbidden fruit can be a coworker who is married or a former boyfriend or girlfriend from high school. This forbidden fruit may even be a former addiction. It is knocking at your door, waiting with anticipation for you to let it in.

As a married person, I know that there are moments within our married journey when it seems our other half is not interested. Just because our other half seems not interested in us does not give us permission to seek after someone else. Every couple swim through rough waters now and then. We must maintain our integrity and trust in the God of the impossible.

> *"Then the LORD God called to Adam. Where are you?" (Genesis 3:9 NKJ)*

Adam and Eve had sewed for themselves clothing made of leaves in an attempt to hide their scars. They had disobeyed their Father's command by eating what they should have not even considered touching. All around them were trees filled with delicious fruits. These trees were not off limits to the couple. However, instead of remaining contempt, they ventured into the forbidden.

Could God now love them after they had done what He explicitly forbade them not to eat? Can God love you and me even when we mess up and fall flat on our faces? How can He love us if even our families have abandoned us?

In the book of Romans 6:23, we get an amazing glimpse of who God really is: "For the wages of sin is death, but the free gift of God is eternal life through Christ Jesus our Lord" (NLT).

After what they had done, the couple were probably suffering from anxiety and fear. They feared for what would be the outcome of their defiant attitude. Would they be zapped by lightning? Would they be squashed like bugs? Many were the fearful thoughts that kept appearing in their minds. Suddenly they heard God walking towards them, so they hid.

Can you hear the Creator calling them? "Adam, Eve, where are you?" It is hard for me to imagine that this was the first time God ever visited His children. Certainly, Adam and Eve were familiar with their Father's walk and talk. "Adam, Eve, I want to spend time with you..." is what I believe God would have said to our first parents at the garden.

Did God not know where His children were? Is He not omniscient? When my children were smaller, we would play "hide and go seek". "I will count to ten and you hide, okay?" were my directions for my girls. "One, two, three." The counting began as I could hear my children scamper to find a good hiding place. At that moment there were not many places to hide, since we were living in a two-bedroom apartment. When the counting was over, I would yell, "Ready or not, here I come." A quick glance of the living room revealed my daughters were hiding behind the long crimson curtains. I slowly made my way to the curtains. However, as a good father, I was going to play with them a little.

"Celina? Jessie? Where are you?" I would call as I approached their hiding place. The closer I got to the curtain, the more I would yell, "Celina, Jessie, where are you?"

Suddenly the curtain began to move as I heard the girls giggle. "Where are you?" I would check under the dining table, then under the rug. "Celina, Jessie, where are you?" Their laughter got louder and louder when all of a sudden, I would hear a cry is from behind the curtains: "Over here, Daddy."

When my daughters were hiding, I knew exactly where to find them. Their little feet kept moving, allowing the curtains to sway side to side. Since my girls love to play with Daddy, I let them believe I had no clue as to their whereabouts. When Adam and Eve hid, God knew exactly where they were. Our heavenly Father is not only a good Father. He is a great Father-ever loving, ever gracious, ever merciful, and ever playful.

There is nothing you can do that will stop God from loving you. His love for a fallen race transcends all human logic. His love for you and me goes deeper than the deepest sea. It reaches higher than any visible star. It is as wide as the east is to the west. He loves you because you are His child.

Adam and Eve realized how pointless it was to hide from God. Gradually they came out from their hiding place, and Adam said, "I heard you in the garden, and I was afraid. So I hid."[3] It is as if he was saying, "We did not want you to see our nakedness. We have messed up. We have disobeyed your commands. Our guilt got the best of us, so we hid from You."

What followed was a dialogue between the Creator and the created. Instead of taking the blame, Adam pointed his finger at his beautiful wife. It is at the garden where the blame game was born, and the torch of this game has been passed on from generation to generation.

Do you remember when God gave them clear instructions about which fruit is permissible to eat? "You may freely eat the fruit of every tree in the garden—except the tree of the knowledge of good and evil. If you eat its fruit, you are sure to die."[4]

---

[3] Genesis 3:10 (NIV)
[4] Genesis 2:16-17 (NLT)

When our first parents disobeyed God and ate of the forbidden fruit, their punishment should have been death. God did warn them. Adam and Eve were conscious of the punishment: death! When they chose to disobey, it must have broken our heavenly Father's heart. Adam and Eve knew the rules. They knew of the consequences of eating what was forbidden. A heavy, dark cloud rested upon their hearts, as they feared their deserved punishment.

The Bible says that "God is love" (1 John 4:8 NIV). It is at this precise moment of their lives, at this juncture, that Adam and Eve and all of humanity learned what it means to be saved by grace. Our loving God did not give His children their just punishment. Instead, someone else took their spot and died on their behalf.

> *"And the LORD God made clothing from animal skins for Adam and his wife"*
> *(Genesis 3:21 NLT).*

God gave our first parents the gift of grace by allowing an animal to be sacrificed on their behalf. I believe this animal to have been a lamb. This lamb pointed to the Savior who is also called the "lamb of God, who takes away the sin of the world!" (John 1:29 NIV).

God took away their clothing made from leaves and replaced it with clothing made from an innocent animal. Their former attire symbolized their righteousness, and they were found guilty by wearing it. This awesome God of the impossible took off their righteousness and clothed them with a gift, the gift of grace and eternal life through Jesus Christ:

> *"For the wages of sin is death, but the free gift of God is eternal life through Christ Jesus our Lord." (Romans 6:23 NLT)*

Every time you and I commit a sin and disobey God's word, we deserve to die. Except that the God of the impossible did the impossible for us on Mount Calvary. He has given us a gift. We do not deserve this gift. It was his love for us that compelled God to freely give it. It costs us nothing. Yet it did cost Him His life. It is the gift of grace. The gift of eternal life. When we come to Jesus, with the weight of guilt on our backs, feeling defeated, or with a sense of worthless, God reminds us of how much we really are worth to Him. You and I have been purchased by His blood. We were slaves to sin, but now we are His (read I John 1:18-19). With God we are free to live the life He intended for us to live, a life of happiness. A life of abundance. A life of impossibilities. All credit goes to our God who is the God of the impossible.

This awesome God is calling out to you today saying: "Where are you?" Come to Him where ever you may be in life. Give your life to the God of the impossible and find out what great purpose He has for your life.

(1 Kings 1:18 NLT)
"I have made no trouble for Israel," Elijah replied.
"You and your family are the troublemakers, for you
have refused to obey the commands of the LORD
and have worshiped the images of Baal instead.

Repairing the Altar

Elijah was as human as we are, and yet when he prayed earnestly that no rain would fall, none fell for three and a half years! Then, when he prayed again, the sky sent down rain and the earth began to yield its crops. James 5:17-18 (NLT)

Ahab was king over God's chosen people, Israel. According to scriptures, King Ahab ruled Israel for over twenty-two years. His reign was not one of reputable mention, for the Bible describes Ahab as an evil ruler. Scripture even goes on to say that Ahab did more evil than any other king before him (see 1 Kings 16:30). One of the many functions King Ahab was responsible for, was to bring Israel closer to their God. This would be accomplished by fostering an atmosphere of worship, allowing God's priest to hold public worship alongside their King. King Ahab was to lead by example. Instead of being an example to his people, Ahab went the opposite way and married the daughter of a pagan King, Jezreel. Not only did he marry Jezreel, but King Ahab was seduced into bowing down to Baal, a pagan god. We are told that Ahab went as far as building a temple for this false god. The record shows that Ahab did all this to incite God.

We are not told how many years this obstinate king kept on doing evil, but we do know that God sent a messenger to proclaim an important warning for the king and for God's chosen people. Elijah was one of the good guys. He was a prophet of God. Being a prophet meant he was God's mouthpiece. God related a message of importance to Elijah, and he was to go and present himself to the king. While at the king's presence, Elijah was to communicate to the crown a very important message.

One day as the king was meeting with all his important officers discussing the state of the union, who do you suppose walked in? The man of God, Elijah. He was God's prophet. He did not have an appointment. Neither did he send the king an email to announce his coming. Elijah did not mention it on Tweeter either. God's prophet just showed up before the crown. King Ahab was astonished at this man's boldness. The king was even more astonished that no one had even noticed when Elijah entered the palace. Everyone was silent and amazed. Before the king and witnesses stood Elijah, with an important message to impart. It seemed for a moment that time had stood still while God's mouthpiece proclaimed, "As surely as the Lord, the God of Israel, lives—the God I serve—there will be no dew or rain during the next few years until I give the word!" (1 Kings 17:1 NLT).

Who Was Elijah?

The Bible describes Elijah as a man with many flaws. He was like you and me, except that he was a man of prayer. As a boy, I was taught at school the Lord's Prayer and Hail Mary. Every morning before class began, we would stand up and recite them. Learning these prayers would serve as a spring board that would catapult me to my journey with the God of the impossible. It was during this journey that I learned the value of prayer. When we pray, we are actually opening our hearts to our best friend, God.

My journey has taught me that prayer is more than just repeating the same things over and over until my face turns blue. Prayer is communicating with God by expressing my thoughts and feelings. Prayer is allowing God to know my sense of gratitude for what He has done in my life, and for what He will continue to do. We can never exhaust God with our prayers. On the contrary, He loves it when we come to Him. He is never too busy to hear your concerns. God is never worn out of listening to you. Come as you are and communicate to your heavenly Father, through prayer.

Elijah came into the presence of Ahab without even being noticed by the king's staff. He delivered God's message to the king, and just like that, he was gone. Elijah left the king's presence without any commotion. No one stopped him as Elijah entered the palace, and no one stopped him as he exited. God's servant was not deterred by the king, or the king's guardsmen. This fearless prophet knew that his obedience to God's word would bring upon him only success.

Many are the promises made to Israel as a nation. These promises certainly are relevant to us today. We are God's children. When we obey God, success follows.

Just before Moses died, he gathered all Israel together to remind them of the many blessings God has for those who obey His commands. We read in Deuteronomy 28:13:

> *"If you listen to these commands of the LORD your God that I am giving you today, and if you carefully obey them, the LORD will make you the head and not the tail, and you will always be on top and never at the bottom." (NLT)*

Baal

When Elijah stood before King Ahab to proclaim a drought for all Israel, the prophet understood that he would be labeled by the king and his staff as an insubordinate rebel. For the faithful few who still loved and followed the almighty God, following the steps of an idolatrous king was not an option.

The Israelites had abandoned their true God and instead worshiped a pagan god named, Baal. This pagan god was believed to have total control of rain and storms.[5] Baal was in control of the weather and vegetation. According to oral transmission, a story was told that Baal had grandparents named El and Asherah. Asherah was the mother god, and El was the father of all the gods. El had little to do with the affairs of men. Baal had an enemy god named Mot, "death."[6] Why is this significant to the story? The key element of the plot has to do with the drought that was announced to King Ahab, ruler of the Northern Kingdom, that neither rain nor dew would be present in his kingdom for several years except by Elijah's word.[7] Elijah came to discredit Baal and give all the credit to the real God of Israel, Creator of heaven and earth, God of the impossible.

Searching for Food

For the past three years, Samaria was suffering a severe drought. King Ahab was really concerned about his livestock. Basic essentials like water were running out, and food for the animals was in short supply. All the brooks had dried up, and the grass was also dead. Therefore, King Ahab called Obadiah, his trusted servant who was in charge of the palace. Ahab had ordered Obadiah to go out and search for food in order to save the royal horses

---

[5] Jordan, M. (1993). Encyclopedia of gods : over 2,500 deities of the world. New York, Facts on File.

[6] Ferm, V. T. A. (1945). An encyclopedia of religion. New York,, The Philosophical library.

[7] Beck, J. A. (2006). The land of milk and honey : an introduction to the geography of Israel. St. Louis, Mo., Concordia Pub. House.

and mules. King Ahab divided the land between him and Obadiah while they searched for food and water.

Scripture tells us that Obadiah was a faithful servant of the Lord. At one time Obadiah saved one hundred of God's prophets, by hiding them fifty to a cave. While in seclusion, Obadiah fed God's prophets with burritos and water. Actually it was bread and water. As Obadiah was on the lookout for food and water, out of nowhere he noticed Elijah the prophet coming towards him.

"Elijah, is that you my brother?" asked Obadiah with glee in his heart.

"Yes, it is me, the one and only," replied Elijah. "Go tell king Ahab to meet me here," Elijah told Obadiah. As happy as Obadiah was to see God's prophet, he became quite tense at the thought of appearing before the king to present Elijah's request.

> *"Has no one told you, my lord, about the time when Jezebel was trying to kill the Lord's prophets? I hid 100 of them in two caves and supplied them with food and water." (1 Kings 18:13 NLT).*

Obadiah assured Elijah that the king had been looking for him for the past three years. He also went to explain how the king made every city and town swear that they had not seen God's prophet. Even worse, now Elijah expected Obadiah to appear before the king.

With hesitation, Obadiah probably said to Elijah, "If I appear before the king and tell him that you want to see him, if the king were to agree and show at the meeting place which you requested and you are nowhere to be found, King Ahab will have my head. I assure you, I like my head."

King Ahab was told about Obadiah's encounter with the prophet, and the king agreed to meet Elijah. The moment had arrived when Ahab and Elijah came face-to-face. Without flinching, King Ahab accused Elijah of being a trouble maker.

> *When Ahab saw him, he exclaimed, "So, is it really you, you troublemaker of Israel?" (1 Kings 18:17 NLT).*

I will paraphrase what Elijah responded to Ahab: "I am not the troublemaker... it is you and your entire administration for not obeying the Commandments of the LORD." (1 Kings 18:18). Then Elijah requested to have the king summon all of Israel at the top of Mount Carmel for a showdown.

On Mount Carmel

King Ahab invited all of Israel to the top of Mount Carmel. He also invited all the priests of Baal and the priests of Ashera (850 in all) to the top of the mountain. It was time to settle once and for all who the real God of Israel was: the one and only God. The God of the impossible was about to make Himself tangible by an amazing display of His power.

Elijah approached all of Israel with a heavy heart. He knew that Israel was playing with fire as they could not make up their own mind which deity to follow. God's prophet asked them a question followed by a direct order.

> *"How much longer will you waver, hobbling between two opinions? If the LORD is God, follow him! But if Baal is God, then follow him!" But the people were completely silent." (1 Kings 18:21 NLT)*

How sad it is when we lose sight of God, our Creator, our Redeemer, and our Friend. How sad when we replace Him with wealth, fame, or for any other material objects. When Israel was asked by Elijah to choose a side, to choose between God or Baal, no one responded, or spoke up. Not one person stood up for the God of the impossible. Everyone froze and did not dare to choose a side.

My friends, in this life we have been granted, we must make a choice. We must choose between the God of the impossible, Creator of heaven and earth, and a false god. This false god offers us temporary happiness, which will only result in pain, frustrations, and eventually eternal death. We cannot be on the fence. When it comes to choosing God, there are no fences. Choose today to serve the Lord your God, and you will never regret it.

Elijah was probably disappointed and wondered how the crowed could be so frivolous. Nevertheless, Elijah was there on a mission from the Lord. He must remain focused. Elijah turned to all the priests of Baal and Asherah and directed them to choose a bull for a sacrifice. Once the bull had been killed and cut to pieces, its different parts should be placed on top of the wood, which was on the altar. Then they were directed not to start a fire for the offering. The false prophets were to call upon their god(s) and plead to them to rain fire upon the sacrifice. Elijah would do the same and "The god who answers by setting fire to the wood is the true God!" (1 Kings 18:24 NLT)

Showdown

> *"So they prepared one of the bulls and placed it on the altar. Then they called on the name of Baal from morning until noontime, shouting, "O Baal, answer us!" But there was no reply of any kind. Then they danced, hobbling around the altar they had made." (1 Kings 18:26 NLT)*

Elijah was bewildered with amazement as these false prophets cried out to their false god. They cried out from morning until noon, with no response, no success. Baal's prophets made fools of themselves by "leaping and writhing and screaming"[8] while at the same time tearing out their

---

[8] Cogan, M. (2001). <u>1 Kings : a new translation with introduction and commentary</u>. New York, Doubleday.

own hair and cutting their own flesh. They cried to their god so as to obtain the help they so desperately need. Despite their efforts, there was but silence. There was no voice. No one answered. There was complete silence in the midst of chaos. From the absence of a voice and absence of an answer, God's people realized that there was no one paying attention to the pleas of Baal's prophets. This, of course, was due to the fact that Baal does not exist. Baal is a false god. When you pray to a false god, all you get is absence and silence.

Elijah had had enough of these clowns jumping up and down, lacerating themselves with knives. As these false prophets began to fall one by one like flies, Elijah retorted, "You'll have to shout louder," he scoffed, "for surely he is a god! Perhaps he is day dreaming or is relieving himself. Or maybe he is away on a trip, or is asleep and needs to be wakened!" (1Kings 18:27 NLT). Elijah was very funny.

Aren't you glad that our God never sleeps and is always watching over us? The book of Psalm 121 serves as a reminder that our God always watches over us.

> *I look up to the mountains—does my help come from there?*
>
> *My help comes from the LORD, who made heaven and earth!*
>
> *He will not let you stumble; the one who watches over you will not slumber.*

Indeed, he who watches over Israel never slumbers or sleeps.

The LORD himself watches over you! The LORD stands beside you as your protective shade. (Psalm 121:1-5 NLT)

"Then Elijah called to the people, "Come over here!" They all crowded around him as he repaired the altar of the LORD that had been torn down." (1 Kings 18:30 NLT)

Elijah invited everybody to come near to him while he prepares the sacrifice for the true God of Israel. As we read 1 Kings 18:21, we find Elijah pleading with God's children by speaking to their conscience. He pleads with them to turn from their idolatry. Elijah urged Israel to mend their broken relationship and to return to the Lord. His question to the people had to do with their limping or leaping between Adonai (Lord) and Baal. He was inviting them to draw near to the Lord. It wasn't that the people were nearing or drawing back to Elijah but to God. They had seen the false prophets of Baal and Asherah dance and lacerate themselves until they had no more strength left in them. They had seen that their false god could not answer. Now it was time for them to see the God of the impossible at work. With trembling, the people slowly made their way to Elijah.

Then with reverence Elijah repaired the altar of the Lord, this same language is used in Jeremiah 19:11. God will not repair or heal his people if they continue in their evil ways. This broken-down altar was once a place of true worship. At one point, God's chosen people worshiped there. They worshipped the God of the impossible in the middle of the false god, Asherah which was symbolized by the trees.[9] For a long time God's chosen people had abandoned their place of worship. They permitted Jezebel to destroy the altar of the Lord, and instead worshipped Baal. Today as in the past is a time for reformation. God's faithful remnant has been called to do the work of Elijah and to restore worship to the true God. Many have abandoned their evening worship for a sports game on TV. Many have left their morning prayers because they are too busy running the rat race. It is time that today's homes heal their broken altars and also heal their relationship with their Creator and Sustainer.

As Elijah invited Israel to come near him, all the people approached him. It was time to repair the altar of the Lord that had been destroyed. Elijah took twelve stones as a symbol of the tribes of Jacob, whom God's word spoke to him, saying, "Israel shall be your name." He built with the stones an altar in the name of the Lord. God's prophet Elijah made a trench all around the altar large enough to contain about three gallons of water. Then he collected some wood and stacked the wood on the altar. He killed a young bull, cut it in pieces, and set it upon the wood.

---

[9] Ferm, V. T. A. (1945). <u>An encyclopedia of religion</u>. New York,, The Philosophical library.

He looked at his spectators and said, "Fill four jars of water and pour it on the burnt offering and on the wood."

He then asked them to repeat the procedure, and they did it again. He said do it a third time and they did it a third time. The quantity of water was so much that it came falling down from the sacrifice around the altar and filled the trench until it was overflowing.

When our children were small, we would love to go camping at least twice in a summer. My children would bring their dolls and our dog, Rocky. My wife had always been the expert at setting up camp while I would go and buy wood for our fire pit. There is nothing better than to be around the fire in the evening telling stories to my children while roasting marshmallows. We love camping, except on rainy days. If you have ever gone camping on rainy days, you know how difficult it is to light the fire pit. Not only is it difficult but nearly impossible to start a fire when everything around you is soaking wet.

By allowing the altar, the wood and the sacrifice to be soaked with water, Elijah was making a point. It is impossible for a sacrifice to catch fire while it, and everything else around it was saturated with water. Totally impossible, but then again, Elijah wanted his crowd to remember that with God nothing is impossible.

> *Elijah came to the altar, lifted his hands*
> *to God and pleaded to God by saying, "O*
> *LORD, God of Abraham, Isaac, and Jacob,*

prove today that you are God in Israel and that I am your servant. Prove that I have done all this at your command. O Lord, answer me! Answer me so these people will know that you, O LORD, are God and that you have brought them back to yourself."
(1Kings 18:36-37 NLT)

What followed while Elijah was still praying was nothing short of a miracle. Immediately fire descended from heaven, consuming the bull, the wood, and the altar. The altar was consumed! Every stoned that was placed one on top of each other was forever gone, consumed by the God of the impossible. Wait! Our God was not finished. Do you remember all that water that was poured on the sacrifice, the water that ran down to the trench which was dug up by God's people? All the water was licked (consumed) by the fire that the God of the impossible sent.

Our God, the God of the impossible, is real. There is no other like Him. He is our God, and He loves to answer when we call upon Him. When we search for Him with all our hearts, know that the God of the Impossible is near and will reveal Himself to you.

"When you pray, I will listen. If you look for me wholeheartedly, you will find me."
(Jeremiah 29:12-13 NLT)

Saved by Grace

Someone came to me with the false claim that there was no grace in the Old Testament, to which I replied, "my dear friend, your statement tells me that you have not read the Old Testament."

This story of Elijah is a great example of grace in the Old Testament. Allow me to explain. God's people had abandoned their true God for a false one. They had broken God's commandment by allowing another god to take the place of the real God (Exodus 20:3). Therefore, since Israel had forsaken their one and only true God, they deserved to die: "For the wages of sin is death," wrote Paul, "...but the free gift of God is eternal life through Christ Jesus our Lord." (Romans 6:23 NLT)

God could have sent the fire on His people and wiped them out completely for being disobedient, yet He did not. The fire consumed the sacrifice, which symbolized Jesus Christ. The people should have been annihilated. However, because of God's love towards His children, God allowed for the sacrifice to be consumed. On the cross, Jesus, took our place. We should have died instead of His Son. God loves us with a love that cannot be explained. Now because of His sacrifice, we now have eternal life.

> *"For God loved the world so much that he gave his one and only Son, so that everyone who believes in him will not perish but have eternal life.*

God sent his Son into the world not to judge the world, but to save the world through him." (John 3:16 NLT)

Surrender your life to the God of the impossible and be amazed. All your dreams have been placed in your heart by the God of the impossible. Do not give up on chasing your dreams. Dream big and let God, the God of the impossible, make your dreams come true.

(1 Samuel 16:7 NLT)
But the LORD said to Samuel, "Don't judge by his appearance or height, for I have rejected him. The LORD doesn't make decisions the way you do! People judge by outward appearance, but the LORD looks at a person's thoughts and intentions."

Just a Boy

Years after God rescued the Israelites from Egypt, his people asked for a king to lead them. As God's prophet, Samuel was awakened to the realization that the Israelites had made an enormous mistake by choosing Saul as king, Samuel's heart was engulfed in despair. Outside his quarters the sun was in full splendor, the birds warbled their melodious tunes to the one who created them, and the morning dew was slowly vaporizing until the next day. Although Samuel was filled with remorse and hopelessness, everything indicated that today was a new day.

Samuel was too busy wallowing in self-pity, worried about the state of the nation to realize that today was a brand-new day. Today was the commencement of a new beginning, a new start. Yesterday was forever gone; whatever happened yesterday had been chiseled into the archives of history. We can't do anything about the past except to learn and trust. Trust that God has today in His hands, and if God has your today in His hands, you have nothing to worry about, except to trust in Him.

As painful as the past may seem, we must always learn from it. Our God, the God of the impossible, has something greater and far better for you. Do not imprison yourself by the storms of your past. Today God has set you free. Today God has given you deliverance. Look up, lift your hands to the Almighty and thank Him for purchasing your release. Get up and trust that your heavenly Father, the God of the impossible, the God who sees your tomorrow, has something astounding waiting for you.

Samuel, heard God's instructions loud and clear:

> *"You have mourned long enough for Saul. I have rejected him as king of Israel...fill your horn with olive oil and go to Bethlehem. Find a man named Jesse who lives there, for I have selected one of his sons to be my king...Invite Jesse to the sacrifice, and I will show you which of his sons to anoint for me." (1 Samuel 16:1, 3)*

How in the world would Samuel go to Bethlehem and anoint someone else without King Saul hearing about the matter? King Saul was at one point an inspiring leader to the people of Israel, but now he had become an oppressor, a despot. To obey God was risky enough, but to disobey God had substantial consequences.

God's prophet headed to Bethlehem with alertness and with the promise of a new start. As he entered the town, all the elders were intrigued as to why Samuel would come to town without an announcement of his presence. Why is he here? Does he bring good news or bad news? They wondered as Samuel assured them that his presence came with the assurance of God's peace. "I have come to sacrifice to the LORD", he reassured them. Then he invited Jesse and his sons to the sacrifice.

The hour of truth had finally arrived, and every one of Jesse's boys were asked to pass before Samuel, one by one, as if auditioning for a beauty pageant.

The oldest son appeared before Samuel, and the prophet of the Lord was impressed to say the least. This young man was tall and good looking. In a way he resembled the current king, Saul. Immediately Samuel had thought that God's chosen one was before him. How could anyone not like what they saw? His height, his physique, his charming good looks. Yup-looks like the next king is right before me, right? Then came a crushing blow to Samuel's imperceptive sight, God said to Samuel:

> *But the LORD said to Samuel, "Don't judge by his appearance or height, for I have rejected him. The LORD doesn't make decisions the way you do! People judge by outward appearance, but the LORD looks at a person's thoughts and intentions." (1 Samuel 16:7 NLT)*

The world is enthralled with the appearances. They say you have to have the perfect nose, great plumed lips, and gorgeous eye lashes. Well, you get the picture.

However, our God does not pay much attention to what is on the outside as much as to what is on the inside. Why would He not look at what is on the inside? He created you. He wired you for success, for victories. With God at your side, there are no challenge you can't overcome, no summit you can't reach.

One by one, each of Jesse's sons came, and not one of them was chosen. After becoming fully aware that none of these men were going to be selected, Samuel asked Jesse if he had other children. I can almost hear Jesse mumbling, "Other children? Why would anyone ask about other children when my finest specimen passed before us?"

Jesse looked at Samuel and with disbelief made Samuel aware that indeed there was one more son, but he was only a boy. What could you possibly want with a boy, a shepherd boy? He has more important matters to attend to than to be here! Sheep need to be fed, watched over; as they graze the lush green grass of the area.

> *"...Send for him at once," Samuel said. "We will not sit down to eat until he arrives." (1 Samuel 16:11 NLT)*

Sensing the intense need Samuel had to see his youngest son, Jesse sent a messenger to immediately have David come before God's prophet. We are not told how long Samuel had to wait until David would show.

You know, if I were there, I would not mind the lingering. Maybe while we paused, we could stuff ourselves with, grapes, figs, perhaps some fish, maybe a burrito or two. Not a bad way for killing time after all, "Take your time, David," is probably what I would have said.

Unfortunately, Samuel's orders were simple and straightforward: "Send for him at once. We will not sit down to eat until he arrives."[10] Must you be so unreasonable Samuel? There is plenty of good food to go around.

Samuel was not going to overindulge himself until David, the youngster, the lad, the shepherd boy, passed before him.

Not knowing what was to take place, David sped as fast as his two feet could get him there. Once he arrived, he waited patiently, quietly, wondering why he was summoned by his father. What was so urgent that he had to leave his sheep unattended? Jesse saw his boy and ordered David to pass before the prophet Samuel. When Samuel saw the young man, God sent Samuel a text message: "This is the one; anoint him."[11] Samuel got up from where he was sitting, came to David, and poured oil all over his head. Everyone at the party was watching and wondering what it was that they were witnessing.

---

[10] 1 Samuel 16:11 (NLT)
[11] 1 Samuel 16:12 (NLT)

> *"So as David stood there among his brothers, Samuel took the olive oil he had brought and poured it on David's head. And the Spirit of the LORD came mightily upon him from that day on...." (1 Samuel 16:13 NLT)*

My admiration goes out to David. I am not quite sure how I would have reacted if Samuel had poured oil on me. After God's prophet had done his duty, there was no fireworks show announcing the birth of a new king. No paparazzi taking pictures, no dance galas, no selfies to post on social media, no tweets on Twitter, no musical shows. Nothing, nada.

After Samuel left Bethlehem, David went back to work, back to his sheep and back to his mundane life. He went back to his training ground. Although David did not understand all that had just transpired, he knew the importance of being responsible and finishing his task, no matter how boring it may seem.

During my first year of college, I found myself doing anything and everything just to pay my bills. My supervisors asked me to clean a public bathroom. This restroom was notorious for its haunting sights and smells. Those who used this facility were either drunk or blind. Its users would somehow miss their "mark", and there would be urine and bodily waste all over the floor. The cleaning company that I worked for had many employees, yet somehow no one wanted the task of cleaning such wonderful amenities. Since I was the new guy, I was gladly volunteered by my peers (thank you, guys).

Suffice to say that I am grateful that God gave me a strong stomach.

After saying my prayers and reciting Psalm 23:4, "Even when I walk through the dark valley of death, I will not be afraid, for you are close beside me."[12]

This bathroom was my battle-zone. Everything was a mess. I could remember saying, "Lord, give me one more... minute. One more minute, Lord." When it was all said and done, my boss literally came over to congratulate me for a "job well done." He continued, saying, "In all this city, you will not be able to find such a cleaner public bathroom than this."

Wherever you find yourself, whatever line of work you are doing, remember to give God the glory and do the best job possible for Him. Our God, the God of the impossible will sooner or later reward you for your faithfulness in the little things, no matter how smelly the situation.

God Sees Potential. God Sees a King

Many moons had come and gone. Many birds had sung their morning song. Israel's army was assembling for war, pacing forward, marching to the valley of Elah. Meanwhile

---

[12] Ibid.

the Philistines were radiant with confidence, progressing with poise to Ephes-Dammim.

You ask, why the Philistines were optimistic, and brimming with confidence. Before the battle lines were drawn, before the battle had been won, in their hearts the champagne was overflowing and the confetti was falling. To them the celebration had just begun. In their midst was the champions of champions, a fearsome warrior, a fighter, a giant of a man. The Bible describes him in this way:

> *"Then Goliath, a Philistine champion from Gath, came out of the Philistine ranks to face the forces of Israel. He was a giant of a man measuring over nine feet tall! He wore a bronze helmet and a coat of mail that weighed 125 pounds. He also wore bronze leggings, and he slung a bronze javelin over his back. The shaft of his spear was as heavy and thick as a weaver's beam, tipped with an iron spearhead that weighed fifteen pounds. An armor bearer walked ahead of him carrying a huge shield." (1 Samuel 17:4-7 NLT)*

As we journey through this highway of life, we are faced with many daunting, life-changing challenges. These are crisis that test us to the core and that are of mammoth proportions. How do we face these giants? What weapons do we have at hand to eliminate these colossal fears that serve as hindrances?

God's army was not acting their part. They were horrified, too afraid to even look beyond this enormous giant. For forty days, two times a day, this titanic of a man paraded himself, hurling insults at God and at His terror-stricken warriors.

> *"I defy the armies of Israel! Send me a man who will fight with me!" (1 Samuel 17:10 NLT)*

Goliath took pleasure in his distinguished abilities and stature. "Send me a man. There is no need for much blood shed." Goliath was saying, "Lets save our time and efforts. Just send me a man to fight with me."

Where was Israel's champion? Where was that knight in shining armor who would with one blow defeat this Philistine? Israel's soldiers were crippled with anxiety. Fear had gripped them to the point of squeezing out their will to fight.

Saul, Israel's king, was nowhere to be seen or heard. With every passing hour, he realized how dire this situation was becoming. When Saul was first introduced to the Israelites, he was described as "...head and shoulders above anyone else" (1 Samuel 10:23 NLT). At first Saul was a humble man, but power had turned him into an arrogant, people-pleasing king. Now here he was, mentally shattered, a coward, trembling before Goliath.

David was summoned once more by his father, Jesse. Leaving his sheep, David swiftly made his way to his home. His three oldest brothers, Eliab, Abinadab, and Shammah, had already enlisted in the army and were at the battle front. Wanting to know how his children were doing and how the war was advancing, Jesse sent David with food and gifts for his brothers and captains of the army.

Even though Jesse thought to send David on an errand, God was behind the scenes sending David on a mission.

Upon David's arrival, Israel's army was heading to the valley, where they would once again be face-to-face with the Philistines and their champion. Marching ahead, demoralized and disheartened as they approached step by step, their hearts sank as in times past. Ahead of them stood Goliath, towering above his peers, dominating, hulking, and as times past throwing insults at Israel's army and at Israel's God.

> *"As soon as the Israelite army saw him, they began to run away in fright." (1 Samuel 17:24 NLT)*

Why were they too scared? What motivated them to run and hide? These men were Saul's highly trained soldiers, and not one stayed to fight the challenger. All the fighters were too scared, too frightened, maybe even too shocked to hear Goliath belittle them and belittle their God, one more time.

Saul had turned his back on God by lying and disobeying God's orders. If only he would have been obedient, victory would have been his. The monarch could have easily received a pardon if he had confessed with all his heart and abandoned his ways. However, here we find him, hiding, running away from his fears and from the God of the impossible.

Fear is an emotional response that gives birth to anxiety causing us to become paralyzed at what we perceive might happen. When we open the door to fear and anxiety, we are inclined to lose focus of reality, and our reaction is simply to run and hide instead of looking up and fighting.

How do we fight? By going on our knees and remembering God's many promises to never forsake us nor abandon us. Here is one example:

> *Do not be afraid or discouraged, for the LORD is the one who goes before you. He will be with you; he will neither fail you nor forsake you." (Deuteronomy 31:8 NLT)*

Once you have come to God and placed all your fears at the foot of the cross, don't look back. Don't look away. Don't look down. Instead, look up. God is bigger than your dilemmas. Face your fears, knowing that the God of the impossible goes before you.

After hearing this giant challenge God's army, young David was fuming and asked, "Who is this pagan Philistine that he is allowed to defy the armies of the living God?" (1 Samuel 17:26 NLT)

David's outlook on life was different from all his equals. Instead of running, looking for an escape route, he came to the source of strength and valor: God.

Standing before King Saul, David assured him that he would go out and fight Goliath. The king responded in this way.

> *"Don't be ridiculous! There's no way you can fight against this Philistine. You are only a boy, and he has been in the army since he was a boy!" (1 Samuel 17:33 NLT)*

Have you ever shared your dreams with a relative or a close friend, only to be shattered by their pessimism? David was an optimist. He displayed courage and optimism before King Saul and Saul's army. Why would he not be an optimist? He knew God was on his side. He understood that even if he was younger and smaller than this massive being, God was his heavenly Father and David was His son. If God created the universe just by speaking it, David understood that no problems David faced were too big for God.

If God can create something out of nothing, God can cast your fears away. Look up. Stand up. Fight. Do not quite until you have achieved your dreams. Fight. You are not alone. The God of the impossible is on your side.

It's His Battles, Not Yours

During his interview with King Saul, David maintained a positive attitude. His faith in God was unshakable, and he would not be moved or discouraged. David acknowledged that it is important to always disengage with their negative comments. Since Saul was playing the pessimist, this young lad understood that it is best to always remain positive and never under any circumstance take their words personally. There are moments where it is best to run away from all the pessimists in your life.

Armed with a staff, a sling, five smooth stones and most importantly with God, David was about to give us a lesson of trust and faith. We must trust in a Being bigger and stronger than all of us. We cannot see God, but all creation speaks to us of Him. God is there to sustain and be our guide. In our darkest moments of life, God holds us in His arms and bids us to trust in Him.

> *Trust in the LORD with all your heart; do not depend on your own understanding. Seek his will in all you do, and he will direct your paths. (Proverbs 3:5-6 NLT)*

One look at David, and this monster of a man was insulted. King Saul was the tallest among his men. He should have been fighting Goliath. Instead Saul sent this boy to battle. "Is this a joke?" Goliath thought out loud.

> *"Am I a dog," he roared at David, "that you come at me with a stick?" And he cursed David by the names of his gods. (1 Samuel 17:43 NLT)*

When our giants mock us and laugh at us, remember, this battle belongs to the Lord. David came in the name of the Lord and said, "Today the LORD will conquer you." (1 Samuel 17:46 NLT). When we allow the Lord to conquer our fears and anxieties, we will become what He intended us to be. This battle you are facing belongs to the Lord. The God of the impossible will win your battles. He has won the ultimate battle for you and me, while he hung on the cross at Calvary.

> *"The LORD does not need weapons to rescue his people. It is his battle, not ours. The Lord will give you to us!" (1 Samuel 17:47 NLT)*

Suffice to say that David won the battle because he realized that every battle we face belongs to the LORD. He will never let us be defeated. He is, after all, the God of the impossible.

(2 Samuel 9:1 NLT)
One day David asked, "Is anyone in Saul's family still alive-anyone to whom I can show kindness for Jonathan's sake?"

Living Like Royalty

King David spread himself across the floor. Filled with gratitude, he communed with God. His face gleamed like the rising of the sun, his eyes, red and watery. His heart was filled with endless joy. Out of his mouth came a soft warm utterance: "Thank You." Hope and peace reigned in his heart as he contemplated all that God had done for him.

> "Who am I, O Sovereign LORD, and what is my family, that you have brought me this far?" (2 Samuel 7:18 NLT)

How can it be that just a few years ago, David was just a shepherd boy? Who could have imagined that this shepherd boy would one day be king of Israel, ruler over God's chosen people? Appreciation for the opportunity granted to him filled his heart. While meditating on God's kindness to David, he soon remembered his promise to his best friend, Jonathan.

Friends are a gift from God. We must discern between a true friend and an acquaintance that calls himself your friend. The Bible recalls the encounter between David and Jonathan.

> *"After David had finished talking with Saul, he met Jonathan, the king's son. There was an immediate bond of love between them, and they became the best of friends. Jonathan made a special vow to be David's friend, and he sealed the pact by giving him his robe, tunic, sword, bow, and belt." (1 Samuel 18:1, 3-4 NLT)*

Sitting upon his throne, King David was surrounded by his most-trusted men. The king had one inquiry in mind, and he needed his best and finest to find the answer. The conversation probably went like this, "Is there anyone of King Saul's family alive?" (2 Samuel 9:1 NLT). "When Jonathan was living, we made a pact to show kindness to ourselves and our loved ones." The answer came swiftly by one of the kings trusted confidant's. "There is a man named Ziba, he was one of king Saul's servants, and at the moment he provides aide to one of king Saul's relatives."

The kings' heart leaped for joy at the thought that there might be someone from King Saul's family alive and well. Ziba was brought in before the king. Not knowing why he was summoned by King David, Ziba was nervous. He could only speculate what king David might want to do to a servant of the King's bitterest enemies.

> *The king then asked him, "Is anyone still alive from Saul's family? If so, I want to show God's kindness to them." Ziba replied, "Yes, one of Jonathan's sons is still alive. He is crippled in both feet." (2 Samuel 9:3 NLT)*

Imagine what must have bolted across Ziba's mind. "Wait, the king is not going to kill me? He wants to show God's kindness to my master Mephibosheth. This has to be a trap?" Ziba let the king know that a son of Jonathan remained. However, he might as well be dead. God has punished him. He is crippled.

Being crippled in those days was considered a curse. It was one way of showing how hated the crippled was by God. The mindset was that if you were a cripple, it was because God was punishing you for a sin committed against Him. The Bible gives us some indication as to how and why Mephibosheth was lamed.

> *"(Saul's son Jonathan had a son named Mephibosheth, who was crippled as a child. He was five years old when the report came from Jezreel that Saul and Jonathan had been killed in battle. When the child's nurse heard the news, she picked him up and fled. But as she hurried away, she dropped him, and he became crippled.)" (2 Samuel 4:4 NLT)*

Upon hearing that Saul and Jonathan had been killed, Mephibosheth's babysitter (nurse) panicked and considered hiding the child before David could find him and exterminate the boy. Mephibosheth was only five years old when his baby sitter picked him up and made a run for it to a place named Lo-debar (in Hebrew this means "no grass"). Lo-debar was situated east of the Jordan River.

In a way I can sympathize with Mephibosheth. When my parents decided that my country of birth was too dangerous to live in, we all escaped to Belize. I was six years old when my dad found a note on our front yard, stating that we had to leave our country, or the death squadron would be coming for us. During the civil war in El Salvador, a secret police force was formed to assassinate, torture and even performed forced disappearances of persons or families. Dad mentioned to me that "death squads" were not known much. However, everything changed on March 24, 1980. Archbishop Oscar Romero was assassinated by a sniper, as he performed mass.

El Salvador had plunged itself into a civil war. For twelve long years many innocent people lost their lives. One night I was in the front seat of my dad's car as we were headed home from the capital city of San Salvador. We were on a roundabout heading towards my hometown of Quezaltepeque, when I recall seeing many militia men stopping a public bus. These men got on the vehicle searching for a suspect. It did not take long for my dad and me to hear shots fired and people screaming. Dad shoved my head to the floor of the car and demanded that I not get up. Our car raced out of the roundabout, and Dad steered the car finding refuge at a hotel far from that neighborhood. As we were frantically making our way out of the crime scene, I would raise my head and try to take a peek at what was evolving before us.

For years Mephibosheth tried to lay low, out of sight, not wanting anyone to know where he was hiding for fear that word might reach the king. If a current king wanted to keep his throne safe, execution of any close relative of the previous king was their choice move. Since Mephibosheth was King Saul's direct grandson, making him the next heir for the crown, Mephibosheth knew that it was only a matter of time before King David killed him.

That is the reason he was hiding out. He would rather live the remainder of his life as a beggar, a scrounger. He would sooner be left alone than be condemned to death for something he had no say about. He did not ask to be Jonathan's son. He did not ask to be King Saul's grandson. He was only a child when he was dropped by his nurse as they were running for dear life. Now he was alone, with no family to love and be loved by. Feeling sorry for himself, Mephibosheth thought of himself as a nobody, a parasite, a burden to society and to his only loyal friend, Makir.

Perhaps you have felt the way Mephibosheth was feeling. Perhaps you thought of yourself as underserving. Perhaps you have felt unloved. Many times you have even considered yourself a burden to society. Just remember that the King of the universe came down to this miniscule of a planet and humbled Himself by clothing his divinity with humanity. He was willing to leave His throne so you can have a home. He was beaten and bruised so you can live a purposeful life. God gave His life so that you and I can live, live eternally with Him. You are valuable to Him.

> *"Don't be afraid!" David said. "I intend to show kindness to you because of my promise to your father, Jonathan. I will give you all the property that once belonged to your grandfather Saul, and you will eat here with me at the king's table!" (2 Samuel 9:7 NLT)*

As Mephibosheth was slowly transported to the very presence of King David, his demeanor before the king was one of uncertainty. He was scared to the point of shaking. While making his way to the king, he had time to contemplate how the king would kill him. King David noticed his appearance and realized how scared Mephibosheth was. Mephibosheth was assured by the king that he had no reason to be afraid.

Like Mephibosheth, we tend to run away from God and seclude ourselves from Him. We are inclined to let fear dictate our actions. Don't run away from God. We cannot hide from Him. He is continuously endeavoring to win our trust in Him. Our God, our Creator, is madly in love with you. You are His child. He created you and wants to establish an intimate relationship with you. Will you give Him a chance? He wants to show you His kindness.

David wanted Mephibosheth to experience God's kindness. God, after all, had been kind to David, and now the king wanted nothing more than to see one of King Saul's relatives experience what he (David) was experiencing. We read in Psalms 34:8 (NLT), "Taste and see that the LORD is good. Oh, the joys of those who take refuge in him!"

When you allow God into your heart and authorize Jesus to be your Savior and King, you will never be the same again. Within you is awakened a sense of why you were brought to this planet and a desire to be all that God intended you to be.

> *Mephibosheth bowed respectfully and exclaimed, "Who is your servant, that you should show such kindness to a dead dog like me?" (2 Samuel 9:8 NLT)*

Where we come from, our dog was just a dog. It was useful for warning strangers to stay away from our property, but it was just a dog. It lived outside our four walls and was never allowed to come inside. We never considered it part of our family. We never allowed it to eat from our dish. We never kissed it, and we certainly never gave it our last names. A dog is just a dog.

When we moved from El Salvador to Canada, my parents and I were a little disturbed at how animals (pets) were allowed to live inside the home along with the rest of the family. We had never seen a person walking behind their dog with a leash and a plastic bag to pick up the dog's waste. It was a culture shock for all of us.

Having been raised in North America, I understand the importance of having a pet. When we were living in Michigan, my children asked us for a dog. As students, we could not afford a pet. We were very tight on finances. Another reason for not getting a pet was the possibility of a major move to Colorado. We decided to put a hold on getting a pet until our move was complete. Upon moving to Colorado, our children would not let us rest until we got them their desire: a puppy.

Rocky was the name given to this beautiful, playful, white cotton ball. He is a bichon poodle. His personality is cheerful. We do not know what we would do without Rocky. He is very friendly-too friendly I might add. He is a very good watch dog. You see, if thieves ever come to our house, our dog will sit there and watch them take everything.

This is the reason why it is easy for me to understand what Mephibosheth meant when he said to King David, "I am a dog...not just any dog but a dead dog." In other words, what he was saying was, "I am useless to you and anyone else. I am ashamed of myself, and my God has punished me for something I did not do. What could you possibly want from me? I am no good, insignificant, and unworthy of such kindness."

For many years Mephibosheth spent his life fleeing from King David because he was under the assumption that if he was found, King David would kill him. Living alone and in poverty, feeling ashamed, undeserving, and worthless, Mephibosheth was missing out on life.

Have you ever felt the way Mephibosheth felt? I want to remind you that you are royalty. That's right, your heavenly Father is waiting for you to come. The King of kings, Creator of the universe, is waiting for you to realize that you were made for something better. Maybe you spent all your life running away from God. Maybe you are still under the false assumption that God, your God cannot and does not love you. Give yourself to Him. Allow for His will to be done in your life. For He has plans for you, plans that will exceed your imagination. Here is a promise from God to you:

> *For just as the heavens are higher than the earth, so are my ways higher than your ways and my thoughts higher than your thoughts. (Isaiah 55:9 NLT)*

Our God is a selfless God. He is not confined to time or space. Therefore, His thoughts for you go beyond the moment. His purpose for you extends to eternity. We are selfish, thinking of only ourselves while God thinks only of you and your well-being. We think about what we can get out of a relationship while God thinks of what He can give. His limitless goodness and mercy are linked with His plans and purpose for your life, both here and the hereafter.

David made room for Mephibosheth at the king's table and Mephibosheth was treated as one of the king's sons.

You and I are children of God. He showed us this fact when He was willing to come down to us and die on our behalf. Eternal life is ours if we choose Jesus. We now can live a life of peace, a life of freedom because of what Jesus did for us on the cross. Come to Jesus with all your fears and anxieties. Come to Jesus with all your worries and weaknesses. You are loved by the King. Come to Jesus and find out what plans God has for you. Come to the God of the impossible.

(Mark 1:40 NLT)
A man with leprosy came and knelt in front of
Jesus, begging to be healed. "If you are willing,
you can heal me and make me clean," he said.

Heal Me LORD

Have you ever felt unfit to participate in any religious or social activity? Have you ever been told that you are not good enough for God? You are not good enough for society? You are not good enough for your family?

The word of God reveals to us a story that can well be placed in our modern times. The Bible does not give us details about the name of the main character. We do not know if this person is married or single. Where he was from is a mystery. Nothing is said about his age or about his friends and family. One thing we do know about him is that this person had an awful disease known as leprosy.

Since we do not know much about this person except that this person was a male, we will give him a name. Please allow me to introduce you to Bob. Let us use our imagination and pretend that Bob was recently married, and his wife just gave birth to a beautiful baby girl. Bob had a great job, and it paid very well. He was liked at the office, and you could always count on him to talk stories by the cooler. Everyone who came in contact with him, liked him. He was the life of the party. Everything was about to change for Bob. One morning as he got up to shower and prepare to head out for work, his wife saw a strange rash on his forehead.

After inspecting this rash on Bob's forehead, she said to Bob, "Honey, you have a rash on your forehead, and I can't figure out what it is."

After much agonizing, Bob knew exactly what he should do. According to the Levitical law, anyone with a swelling or a rash on their skin had to present themselves to the priests for further examinations. If the priest noticed that the hair in the affected area had turned white, then it was leprosy.

Leprosy was highly contagious, and according to the belief of those days was that it was a curse from God. They say that leprosy attacked the nervous system, damaging a person's ability to feel pain. A leper could accidently walk on nails and not realize it, until his foot got infected. Once infected, his foot got weaker and wasted away.

Society thought and taught that if you had contracted leprosy, it was because God had turned His back on you. It was said that if you had leprosy, God did not love you. If God shunned you from His presence, then you were banned from society, and from living a normal, happy life. If God saw it fit to abandoned you, then society would do the same.

The priest examined Bob's rash. Because his hair had on or near the affected area had not yet turned white, this brought some uncertainties. If the priest was not sure about the rash or swelling of the skin. If the affected area was not more than skin deep, then Bob would be placed under quarantine. He was locked up for a whole week.

Imagine being locked up for a week without the possibility of seeing your loved ones. A week without being with friends. A week without pay? Bills would mount up, yet you are helpless. You can't do anything about your circumstances except cry and pray that all will turn out fine.

After the seven days were up, Bob was brought back before the priest, who would once again examine his rash or swelling. Once the priest determined that Bob's rash had not changed in color or size, Bob was sent for another seven days in quarantine. By then he had spent three full weeks locked up in a solitary room, banned from society. Three weeks without speaking to his wife. Three weeks without seeing his new born baby. Three weeks without hearing words of hope and comfort. Three weeks without feeling a touch of love. No one to caress him. No one to kiss him. No one to encourage him. Three weeks of loneliness and despair. Three weeks of feeling hopeless. Three weeks of feeling useless. His heart was shattered. A sense of abandonment griped his soul. Where was God? Why was this happening to him? These were the questions that enthralled him.

That tantalizing day came when the priest examined Bob one more time and declared him to be "unclean". Since it was the priest's duty to keep the camp healthy, free from decease, it was the responsibility of the priest to expel a leper from their midst. Seeing that God had cast Bob aside to die alone, the priest also made sure that anyone with leprosy, would also suffer the same fate and be cast away from the population. All lepers were banished to the valley of lepers. They were sent there in order to die a slow painful death.

Bob could not come into contact with his family and friends. He could not be out in public. If he was found in public, he must suffer the shame of having rocks hurled at him. It was said that even the air one breathed, was contaminated by the presence of a leper.

Unclean! Unclean! Unclean! This was the cry heard from all who were deemed socially and religiously unfit. The law required that all lepers stay far away from others. They were to tear their clothes to pieces, and with their mouth covered cry aloud, "Unclean!"

Once again, the Bible is silent about the longevity of Bob's absence from society. Probably the author of this biblical story was not concerned on dates. The author of this story was more concerned about you and I knowing that one day Bob heard about this man named Jesus. Bob heard from other lepers that Jesus had given sight to the blind. Jesus made the lame to walk. Jesus gave speech to the mute. At His command, the roaring seas would hush.

As Bob was hearing all the great things about Jesus, Bob began to hope again. *Could it be that Jesus would see me? Could it be that Jesus would want to be close to me?* Questions after questions flooded Bob's mind. *Could it be possible that Jesus could love me?*

One day Bob mustered enough courage to go see this healer called Jesus. How bad could it be? What did Bob have to lose? He already lost all that was dear to him. His only hope was in Jesus.

No matter what you are facing today, come to Jesus. Trust that He is able to make the impossible, possible in your life. Remember, there is nothing impossible for God.

Coming to Jesus is our only hope in life. Others may see trash, but Jesus sees more, something worth more than gold. For Jesus, the value of a person is not found on the outside. All that matters to God, is what is on the inside of a person. How is your heart towards God? Allow Him to come into your life. Permit Him to transform you. Sanction Him to heal you. He loves you with a love that cannot be measured or explained. You are not alone. You are His child. He cares for you. You see, time after time we are reminded by God that to Jesus, our deformities do not matter. Our diseases can't keep Jesus from coming to us. Jesus wants to heal your wounds. Jesus wants to repair your broken heart. Will you allow Him?

Bob wanted nothing more than to see Jesus. Nothing was going to stop him from coming to the Master. Once Bob learned where Jesus could be found, he got up from the hole he was in and headed to his only hope: Jesus.

I can almost hear the cry in his voice as he approached the multitude that thronged around Jesus. Covering his head, Bob slowly made his way to the crowed. With a clamor, Bob warned the crowd of his approaching. "Unclean!" he shouted, "unclean!" The crowed heard the cries, and looked at the direction of Bob.

How could it be? A leper in our midst? They all picked up stones, ready to be hurled at will. They shouted to Bob, warning him of what to expect if he got any closer.

"Stay away from us, you filthy scum," they shouted. "If you come closer, we will have no choice but to stone you."

Bob was not going to be intimidated by all the hurls and insults. He was on a mission to see Jesus.

Make it your mission today to see Jesus. Come to Him just as you are. You are not a mistake. Your beauty is unmatched. You are valuable. You are beyond comparable. You are unique. God brought you here for success, not for failure. Place your life in His hands and move out of the way. Watch Him work in you and for you. Life will never be the same again when you realize that God has your best interest in mind. Let God chisel and mold you into the person you were created to be.

Bob would not stop advancing. People tried their best to keep Bob away from receiving his blessings. Don't allow society to tell you your worth. God paid your value with His blood. You are worth more to God than what gold is worth to us.

I love how people realized the futility in stone throwing, name bashing, and morale-crushing insults. All the insults hurled at Bob did not stop him. Everyone who was with Jesus fled away. They did not want to be contaminated with this disease.

Bob came to Jesus and uttered these words: "If you are willing, you can heal me and make me clean," (Mark 1:40 NLT).

Falling on his knees, Bob, humbled himself and realized that there was one being in the universe who would never turn him down. "I know You can heal me," he said, "but if You are willing, make me clean." What Bob was saying is, "I understand that I am a sinner, abandoned by my community. I am alone. I feel worthless, not deserving of anything. However, there is nothing impossible with You, and You are able to heal me. You are able to make me clean. Here I am. Take my life, my future is in Your hands."

Jesus, not wanting to let Bob suffer any longer and moved with compassion, said, "I am willing, be healed!" (Mark 1:41 NLT)

Our God is a compassionate God. He is concerned about your wellbeing. Others might shove you aside. Some will look down on you. Society may say you "don't belong", but God says, "You are Mine". "You are stunning, beautiful, staggering." This is how God sees you. It does not matter what negatives slurs come out of others. All that matters is that God loves you just the way you are.

Say this phrase to yourself everyday: "I am a child of the King. I am beautiful and resilient. With God by my side, there is nothing I can't accomplish. With God all things are possible.

(Daniel 8:1 NLT)
But Daniel was determined not to defile himself by eating the food and wine given to them by the king. He asked the chief of staff for permission not to eat these unacceptable foods.

14 minutes in Paradise

Daniel and his friends were prisoners of war. They had been taken captive by the powerful Babylonian Empire. Everything that was dear to them had now perished, and now they were being dragged under the hot dessert sun to a country they had never seen before. Goodbye to their mother land, symbol of hope, love, and comfort. Despite their reluctance, they were yanked away to embrace their new reality, their new home. No more were they to see their father and their mother. They were to learn a new culture, eat different foods, and speak a foreign language.

These young prisoners had all the excuses to feel resentful towards their captors for intruding into their lives. As they walked for miles every day under the hot, heavy sun, with their hands bound to the person ahead of them, they had all the time to feel even angry towards their God for not sparing their loved ones or their home. While making their way to Babylon, hungry, tired, and upset, memories of their childhood would permeate their hearts and minds. They would remember all the wonderful stories they had learned about the God of Israel, the God of the impossible.

Where was the God of Abraham? God promised Abraham to make out of him a great nation, and He did. Where was He now? Where was the God of Moses? God brought His people from the land of Egypt with a mighty Hand. He divided the sea so that His people could cross on dry land. He slew Egypt and Pharaoh with ten plagues. Where was He now?

What would you do if you found out that within fourteen minutes your life would come to a violent end? How would you react knowing that a ballistic missile was heading your way? Who would you call?

My alarm went off at 5:00 a.m., as was the routine of every morning. It was Saturday, January 13, 2018. Upon hearing my alarm, I slowly squirmed my way out of bed, trying to be careful to not awake my lovely wife. It was time for morning prayer, some scripture reading, and another morning prayer. It was another beautiful daybreak in paradise (a.k.a., Hilo, Hawaii). After my morning prayer and scripture reading was done, I headed to the shower and began my usual Sabbath morning prep.

Soon the family and I would be heading to church for worship and praise. We have so much to praise Him for. To think that our King and Creator left His entire Kingdom, chose to wrap Himself with humanity and come to this speck of a planet so that you and I should not perish but that we may have eternal life is mind blowing. Our God loves us very much. We can't comprehend or try to explain just how much you and I mean to Him. He chose to leave behind His throne in exchange for a manger, His royal robe for strips of cloth, His scepter for nails. It was those same nails that would hold him to the cross by piercing his hands and feet. He chose to exchange His Royal Crown for a crown of thorns. He gave up all the praises and adoration of His angels for the jeers of a people created by His own hands.

God's love for us is immense and nothing on this planet or anywhere else will make God stop loving us. The apostle Paul writes about God's love in Romans chapter 8:

> *Can anything ever separate us from Christ's love? Does it mean he no longer loves us if we have trouble or calamity, or are persecuted, or hungry, or destitute, or in danger, or threatened with death? (Romans 8:35 NLT)*

> *No, despite all these things, overwhelming victory is ours through Christ, who loved us. And I am convinced that nothing can ever separate us from God's love. Neither death nor life, neither angels nor demons, neither our fears for today nor our worries about tomorrow—not even the powers of hell can separate us from God's love. No power in the sky above or in the earth below—indeed, nothing in all creation will ever be able to separate us from the love of God that is revealed in Christ Jesus our Lord. (Romans 8:37-39 NLT)*

Missile Alert...

Time was running its usual twenty four-hour marathon. My family was almost ready to join me at church when my mother, who was visiting us from Toronto, Canada, came darting into my office with her cell phone in hand.

Looking puzzled she asked, "Son, look at my cell phone and tell me what this means."

I grabbed her phone and wondered why it kept flashing and ringing with the warning: "Emergency Alert, Ballistic Missile Threat Inbound to Hawaii. Seek Immediate Shelter. This Is Not A Drill."

Seconds later, my wife came in with her cell phone in hand. She opened her mouth to say something when we were interrupted by a call to my cell phone. It was someone from church. The caller was frantic as she cried out over the phone, "Pastor, we are all going to die. What should we do?"

I pretended not to understand why she was calling and asked her, "What do you mean we are all going to die?"

Her sobbing could be clearly heard as she whispered, "Didn't you receive the warning on your phone?" Prior to her call, when my mother dashed to my office, I looked at my phone, and there was no alert sent to me.

The caller whimpered out some last questions. "What should I do? Where can I hide?" While she was talking to me, I tried to listen for public sirens. Nothing, no sirens. All was quiet. I quickly turned on my computer and went to CNN and Fox News. Not a word about a missile.

I was perplexed at the utter confusion, so I answered my caller in this way: "Sister, if we are going to die, I can't think of a better place to die at than at church. You live near the church. Why don't you head there now and pray? I will be joining you soon. Please remember that God is still in control." Before I could finish my words to her, my daughter called. She is the eldest of three and was living in Honolulu attending Hawaiian Mission Academy at the time of this chaos.

"Dad, I don't know what to do. Everyone is panicking over here. What should I do?" My heart sank. Tears began to stream out at the thought of not being there to protect my daughter. I assured her that God was still in control, and all we could do is surrender ourselves to Him and pray that He would spare all the population of Hawaii from such a disaster.

"I cannot be with you, but God is, and whatever happens, listen to the instructions of your supervisors."

14 Minutes Before Impact

Prior to this missile alert, there were many talks of possible threats as tensions between the United States and North Korea heightened the possibility of such. The North Korean dictator kept sending us warnings of a missile strike, which prompted much commotion in our community. One thing everyone was certain about was the time it would take for a missile to reach our Islands: fourteen minutes.

For about thirty-seven minutes, disorder reigned in Hawaii as people ran as fast as they could to seek shelter. Some hurried to the mountains, others huddled in their hotel bathroom or closet, and yet others ran out of their building and into the streets not knowing what to do or where to go.

> *Look up into the heavens. Who created all the stars? He brings them out like an army, one after another, calling each by its name. Because of his great power and incomparable strength, not a single one is missing. (Isaiah 40:26 NLT)*

Have you ever tried to count the stars? It is an impossible task, humanly speaking. We must be forever grateful that our God is not human. He is the God of the impossible. He created the stars, and He has given each star a name. It is this same Creator that gave you and me life. He chose you and brought you here for a reason. Like the stars, you are to shine brighter and brighter each day. Even when it seems tiresome, even when you have nothing left in the tank, you shine. We shine brighter when we look up. It is when we look up that we are mindful of the existence of an almighty, all-powerful Creator. It is He who reminds us that we are not mistakes. God has not made a mistake in you. He loves to boast about you. He believes in you simply because He created you. He knows you inside and out. You can say that He has wired you for success. He chose you to shine.

When you look up at the stars, never stop believing, never stop hoping, never stop craving, never stop dreaming, and never stop shining. Even in your darkest hours, never stop shining. To shine means to love, to love those around you even when they do not deserve your love. To shine means to be grateful for life. Every morning you wake up be grateful. This is done by thanking God. Before you get out of bed, thank God. You may wake up feeling low on energy, thank God anyway. Being grateful and thanking God should be put high on your priority list.

Missing Ingredient...

I'll never forget the day Mom decided it was time to travel alone to our country of birth, El Salvador. Traveling alone meant that I would have to attend to the needs of my little brother. I would have to cook, clean, and make sure that he gets to school on time.

One day my brother approached me as I was playing video games and said to me, "Hey, bro, I am hungry."

Feeling a bit responsible, I left my game and started to the kitchen. "Don't worry bro, I'll make us rice, and I'll warm up the leftover chicken."

As a young teenager, I had worked at Mc Donald's, so I felt very confident at making rice. "If I remember correctly," I told myself, "Mom pours the rice in a pot, then adds water. No sweat. How hard can this be?"

Feeling confident, I grabbed a pot and poured enough rice in it till it almost overflowed. After the rice, I added some water mixed with a little bit of olive oil. I turned the stove on and let the rice cook while I continued my game. It did not take long before my brother came to me once more with the look of desperation on his face. He grabbed his belly and reminded me once more that he was hungry. Again, I reassured him that everything was under control, and soon, we were going to eat like kings.

Time was not crawling, it was sprinting, and I had already played about an hour of my favorite video game when my stomach began speaking to me in tongues. I hurried to the kitchen. The water had evaporated from the rice, so I added more water and a bit of oil, and at the same time I remembered to place the chicken in the oven. I decided not to play more video games and instead do something productive: read a book. Once again, my brother came to me with a look of concern. He shook me until I woke up from my slumber. The book was on the ground next to me. I had fallen asleep on the living room sofa. After looking at my food, let's just say that my rice resembled mashed potatoes and my chicken was burned, almost charcoal.

My brother turned out to be wiser than I as he did not want to venture to try my food. My mashed potatoes (rice) were not like how Mom made it. I took a bite of my so-called rice and realized that I had forgotten an important ingredient: salt.

Like cooking, we must choose or determine to add some key ingredients in our lives so that we can face all the hurdles life throws at us. Here are a few ingredients that we must not forget to add in our daily lives.

Choose to Be Optimistic

When your alarm clock goes off early in the morning, or as soon as you open your eyes, choose to be thankful for another day of life. Whisper a prayer filled with gratitude. You can do this on your knees or while you are still lying in bed. Remember that today is another day, whatever happened yesterday is gone, and we can't do anything about yesterday. Today is another day, and your story is still being written. You are the author of your story. With God by your side today will be much different than any other day.

Choose today to be positive, and whenever a negative thought comes to your mind, get rid of it. Always walk with a smile. Smile at your significant other, smile at your children, and smile at your pets if you have them. Just smile. When getting out of bed, remember to make your bed. If you have the time, go to the gym or go for a walk or a jog. Many are the benefits of doing exercise, such as reduction of stress and anxiety to name a few. When you have exercised your muscles, you will notice that your mood has changed for the good (secondscount.org).

You choose what you want to hear and see, but in all this, remember that everything we choose will have a negative or a positive impact in our lives. Surround yourself with music, books, and movies that will only have a positive influence in your daily life.

Choose your friends carefully. Your friends can help you succeed in life, or they can bring you down. That is why you better hang on to those friends and relatives who have a positive impact on you.

If anyone says something negative to you, do not take it personally. You are a child of God. All that should really matter to you is what God thinks of you. You were created for greatness because God is great. He does not make mistakes, and therefore, you are not a mistake.

Choose to Be Resilient.

On May 3, 2018, our beautiful Island of Hawaii, the "Big Island," went through some tough moments as we were hit with with many earthquakes. The biggest quake happened on the following day, Friday, May 4, registering as a 6.9 on the Richter Scale. What happened after were moments of panic and shock as reports of fissures openings in a residential area were making headlines. As the earth opened up, lava began to make its way to the surface, slowly destroying anything in its path.

The lava flows shattered the lives of many on the Island. Although we were uncertain as to when the lava would stop flowing, one thing we did know: God was still in control, and He would take care of us.

Today you can take a drive to the ocean shore and take a stroll on our new black sand beach. God made something beautiful out of all the chaos, just as He will make something beautiful out of your life, no matter how chaotic it may seem at times.

Our beautiful people of Hawaii are very resilient. The island is also as resilient. There is no possible way to hide where the lava flowed, there is no escaping it, yet what remains of the flow is amazing. More amazing than looking at old lava is looking at all those trees stuck in the middle of the flow. They survived all the heat of the lava, and they pulled through despite all the toxic fumes. These trees truly are resilient. We must learn to be resilient and withstand and/or recover from whatever life throws our way.

When the storms of life hit us hard to the point of knocking us down, we go on our knees and pray. The reason we pray is to remind ourselves that God has not left us alone. He has promised us, "Be strong and courageous! Do not be afraid of them! The Lord your God will go ahead of you. He will neither fail you nor forsake you" (Deuteronomy 31:6 NLT). After we have prayed, we stand, for we are not alone. God is leading the way. God goes ahead of us.

Choose to Be Humble

What does it mean to be humble? Before I can answer that question, I want to tell you what it doesn't mean. Choosing to be humble does not mean that you will let everybody walk on you like a dirty old rug. You must not allow that to happen. Remember that you are a child of the King, purchased with His own blood, and therefore, you are valuable. Who you are and who you belong to matters. Always keep your identity in mind. Also remember that your co-workers were also created by the same King. God cares about you as much as He cares about those around you. So, do not belittle anyone. Don't think of yourself as better than anyone. You may be endowed with better skills than everyone around you, and you may work harder than the rest, but let your numbers do the talking for you. Allow your work to be your witness, your agent. Be kind to your fellow humans. Lay aside selfishness and treat others with respect.

Always remember the golden rule Jesus taught us:

> *"Do for others as you would like them to do for you" (Luke 6:31 NLT).*

When it comes to humility, I once heard one of my colleagues say, "The moment you think that you are humble, you have lost it."

In the Bible we read that Moses was:

> *More humble than any other person on earth (Numbers 12:3 NLT).*

There are many instances in the Bible where God requires us to humble ourselves before coming to Him.

> *Then if my people who are called by my name will humble themselves and pray and seek my face and turn from their wicked ways, I will hear from heaven and will forgive their sins and heal their land. (2 Chronicles 7:14 NLT)*

According to the Bible, being humble is all about attitude and having the same mindset of Jesus:

> *"Don't look out only for your own interests, but take an interest in others, too. You must have the same attitude that Christ Jesus had. Though he was God, he did not think of equality with God as something to cling to. Instead, he gave up his divine privileges; he took the humble position of a slave and was born as a human being. When he appeared in human form, he humbled himself in*

obedience to God and died a criminal's death on a cross. Therefore, God elevated him to the place of highest honor and gave him the name above all other names, that at the name of Jesus every knee should bow, in heaven and on earth and under the earth, and every tongue confess that Jesus Christ is Lord, to the glory of God the Father." (Philippians 2:4-11 NLT)

To think that God got off His throne, clothed Himself with humanity and became one of us, so you and I could have eternal life. What an amazing God we serve. He is the God of the impossible, and whatever seems impossible in your life, remember that with God, all things are possible.

(John 4:49-50 NIV)
The royal official said, "Sir, come
down before my child dies."
"Go," Jesus replied, "your son will live." The
man took Jesus at his word and departed.

Faith

Being a parent, I know very well the pain and the sense of helplessness that comes when one of our children gets sick. Just the thought of their suffering makes us wish that we can trade places with our ailing child. Many are the questions that demand answers. Why must my child suffer? What has he or she done to deserve this treatment? Why couldn't I get sick instead? Is anyone listening? Does anyone care?

Have you ever asked those questions? Maybe you are going through something similar with your child at this very moment. The long hours spent by your child's side. The many sleepless nights. The tears shed when no one is watching. This torment is only understood by parents who are going and have gone through this dark, lonely valley of uncertainties.

A couple of days ago, I went to the local cemetery with the purpose of finding a very dear friend who lost his beautiful wife to cancer. After fifty-eight years of marriage, his life-long companion, his best friend, was gone. Life has never been the same for my friend. Yet he has hope and faith. He understands that death is not the end, just a pause.

As I entered the cemetery, I located my friend and made my way to him. When we arrived at his wife's gravesite, we exchanged hugs, handshakes, and words of comfort. What a joy to see how God had given my friend a new mission in life. Every day at a certain time, he is at the graveside where his wife is buried. He is not there only to tend to his emotional needs, but he also waits for his new found friends who share the same pain of having lost a loved one.

While making new friends at the cemetery, we stood by a grave of a young girl. Tears rolled down my eyes when I realized that this child was taken away too soon. After a couple more steps, we saw grave of a young police officer. His life came to an end while he was trying to keep our streets safe for us strangers to enjoy.

In this journey we call life, many are the stories of victories that we have personally witnessed. Far too many are the stories of loneliness and emptiness. I have had the privilege of officiating numerous weddings, and I have had the difficult task of standing by parents as they say their last goodbye to their child.

No one must have to go through the pains of planning the burial of a loved one. In the beginning, it was not God's intentions for us to suffer such heart-wrenching pain.

Miracle In Cana

As Jesus was passing through Galilee, he came to a town named Cana. This is the same place where Jesus turned water into wine (see John 2). The narrative tells us of a nobleman, a government official whose son was ill to the point of death. News of Jesus turning water into wine at Cana was still fresh on everyone's mind. Everyone who took part at the wedding had heard of the miracle and had benefited from drinking this water turned to wine. There were a few at the wedding who had seen this miracle first hand: the servants who were on duty at the wedding.

Upon hearing that Jesus was in Cana, this officer was determined to travel some sixteen miles from the city of Capernaum to Cana. This father was on a mission, and nothing or nobody was going to stop him from standing in the presence of the only one who has the power to speak death away from its victim. I can only surmise that this father, had not yet believed in Jesus. He had heard of the miracle performed in Cana, yet he was in doubt. Perhaps he thought to himself that the only way he would believe in this miracle worker was if Jesus would heal his son.

Once this government official arrived at Cana, he wasted no time in searching for Jesus. With all the buzz floating around about Jesus's return to that region, it was probably easy to find his whereabouts. Upon locating Jesus, the father rushed to His presence urging this miracle worker to follow him and cure his dying son.

I can almost hear his plea: "Please come to Capernaum with me before my son dies." His eyes were probably red and wet from the many tears he had shed for fear of losing his reason for living. "Please, Lord, follow me to my house, or my child will die." He must have repeated this sentence over and over to Jesus in an attempt to gain His compassion.

Jesus read the heart of this suffering father. He knew there was still doubt in his heart. Before satisfying the petitioner's request, Jesus asked him a powerful question: "Unless you see signs and wonders, you will never believe?" (John 4:48 NIV). Perhaps, the father had made up his mind about this miracle worker. It is conceivable from Jesus's question that the only way the father would believe in Jesus was conditional upon his request being granted. Let us be clear about something: the fact that this father came to Jesus implies that he already had some faith. Evidently his faith was not enough to vanish doubt from his heart.

Our God is a God of compassion, mercy, and love. It is written all over the Bible. God's love and compassion for His children is the heart of God's word. It is the gospel, the good news. While passing before Moses, the Lord proclaimed this statement about Himself:

> *"The Lord, the Lord, the compassionate and*
> *gracious God, slow to anger, abounding in*
> *love and faithfulness." (Exodus 33:6 NIV).*

Psalm 111:4 states, "Who can forget the wonders he performs? How gracious and merciful is our Lord." (NLT).

Crazy Faith

Do you have faith? The scriptures define faith as knowing without hesitation that what we hope for will come to reality (see Hebrews 11:1). It is having complete confidence in something or someone greater than us. Faith is trusting that God will grant you the desires of your heart without knowing when or how it will come to pass. Faith is believing in His words no matter the circumstances or obstacles life inflicts upon you. Faith is much more than a word; it is action exhibited by each step you take towards the goals God has placed in your heart.

Back to our Bible story! The boy's father understood Jesus's inquiry. However, time was of most importance. Not knowing if his son was still alive, this government official pleaded one last time, "Lord, come down before my child dies" (John 4:49 NIV). Then out of Jesus's mouth come out the essence of what faith is. Jesus looked at the pleading father and said to him, "Go, your son will live" (John 4:50 NIV). Without hesitation and without asking any questions, the father departed from Jesus's presence and displayed true faith.

As he hurried home, some of his servants were also on the way to meet their master with the great news. I can imagine the conversation went something like this, "Master, your son will live. He is doing fine."

The father of the child asked them, "Around what time did the child feel better?"

> "*It was around one o'clock that his fever vanished*" *(see John 4:52).*

When the child's father realized that it was around the same time Jesus spoke the words "Go back home. Your son will live," (John 4:50 NLT). His faith grew to the point that he and his household followed Jesus.

Our God is the God of the impossible. He is an awesome God. According to science, beaches are made over thousands if not millions of years. On the Big Island of Hawaii, we are basking in the creation of a new black sand beach. God has smiled upon us and has created in a span of days, a new playground for us to enjoy. If our God can create something beautiful from a devastating event in a matter of days, He has the capacity and desire to create something beautiful from the messes of your life. Come to the God of the impossible and watch him do the impossible in your life. As my daughter Celina said to me, "Don't let the imperfections sin brings define who you are. Be the perfect being God created you to be." Trust the God of the impossible.

(Matthew 28:1-7 NLT)

Early on Sunday morning, as the new day was dawning, Mary Magdalene and the other Mary went out to visit the tomb. Suddenly there was a great earthquake! For an angel of the Lord came down from heaven, rolled aside the stone, and sat on it. His face shone like lightning, and his clothing was as white as snow. The guards shook with fear when they saw him, and they fell into a dead faint. Then the angel spoke to the women. "Don't be afraid!" he said. "I know you are looking for Jesus, who was crucified. He isn't here! He is risen from the dead, just as he said would happen. Come, see where his body was lying. And now, go quickly and tell his disciples that he has risen from the dead, and he is going ahead of you to Galilee. You will see him there. Remember what I have told you."

He Is Risen

It was early in the morning, just about the time when the night was at its darkest hour.

Everywhere silence reigned; the night was filled with stars twinkling softly, as if in pain because of the events they had just witnessed, while the moon hung quietly in space seemingly embarrassed by how humanity had treated its own Creator. The only sound that could be heard was that of the soldiers as they discussed the events of that rare Friday afternoon. These strong, brave men were not afraid of the dark, and their duty as sentinels compelled them to stay awake and watch no matter how strange it may have seemed for them to guard the tomb of a dead man. The Roman seal was proof that the tomb had not been touched by intruders. Even if intruders could get near the tomb they would first have to fight against Rome's finest.

The tomb was guarded by seen and unseen armies. Satan and his legions were there, making sure that nothing hampered his plans of ruin. It had been his intentions for Jesus to fall through on His mission, but Satan knew that he had been defeated at the cross. Therefore, one last effort was made by the enemy. His hope was to keep the Son of God forever sealed in that dark and lonely tomb.

Myriads of God's angels were also outside the tomb, waiting patiently for the Son of God to break loose the chains of death. Nothing in the heavens or on earth could bind the Son of God down. His love for the human race is more powerful and stronger than anything or anyone has ever experienced. We simply cannot fathom the immensity of His love for us. Make no mistake about it: Jesus loves you more than anything in this universe. He was willing to give up all so you could gain everything. The Son of God paid the ultimate price. His blood was shed for you, and as a result of His dying on the cross, salvation is now available for the human race.

Suddenly before daybreak, a powerful earthquake was felt across the land. The guards were tossed from side to side until they were cast to the ground. Then a flash of light appeared in the sky. A mighty angel came down from heaven. His face shone like lightning, and his clothing was white as snow. The guards were trained warriors, ever so ready for combat; nothing on earth could scare them except this. The angel sent from God rolled away the stone as if it were a pebble on a sandy beach. With a mighty voice, the angel proclaimed, "Son of God, Your Father calls You."

Poor Roman soldiers. Their hearts were faint, their faces turned pale, and their knees knocked against each other as they fell like dead men to the ground. Then they hear from within the tomb a melodious voice saying, "I am the resurrection and the life."

Out of that dark prison came the same man they had ridiculed just a few days ago. Although the soldiers froze from fright, their minds took them to the events just before the crucifixion. Was not this the same man which an entire battalion ridiculed and chose to teach Him a lesson by beating him then like mad men possessed with evil? They had Jesus stripped of His clothing and placed a scarlet robe on Him. One of those soldiers grabbed a stick and planted it in Jesus's right hand. Still other soldiers put their creative talents to work by making a crown of long and very sharp thorns. Then, with all their strength and hatred, they thrust the crown of thorns on the head of Jesus. As if that was not enough, they all disrespectfully bowed down before him, yelling with one accord, "All hail the king of the Jews!" To make matters worse, and as if all the jeering was not enough, a number of the soldiers began to spit on Jesus's face. Still others grabbed the stick from Jesus's hand and began beating Him with it.

It is hard for me to imagine all that Jesus endured for you and me, yet His love for us is beyond comprehension. He was treated as we deserved to be treated so that we may live eternally with Him. The book of Isaiah clearly prophesied this event: "Yet it was our weaknesses he carried; it was our sorrows that weighed Him down...He was wounded and crushed for our sins. He was beaten that we might have peace. He was whipped, and we were healed!" (Isaiah 53:4-5 NLT)

He Is Alive

Jesus came out of that grave victorious. Nothing could keep Him down. Nothing could separate Him from you. By his victory, we are also victorious because of Him. In everything we do, we are more than conquerors through Jesus our Lord.

Thousands of people flock to Israel just to walk where Jesus walked some two thousand years ago. They visit the Sea of Galilee, where a storm arose and nearly, drowned the disciples. Wet and cold, scared, and feeling helpless, the disciples called on Jesus as He lay fast asleep in the ship. Not realizing that a storm was threatening to swallow the ship, Jesus got up and rebuked the storm and immediately the sea was calm.

Many pray at the garden of Gethsemane, recalling that long night where Jesus fought against the enemy and his army. Jesus was on his knees praying, and He prevailed. The struggle was so intense that Luke describes Jesus as sweating blood and in agony. Here is our answer to being victorious in our everyday trials. We must spend more time on our knees than we do anything else.

Those beautiful Christians walk the road called Via Dolorosa while they imagine God, clothed in humanity, carrying a wooden cross while at the same time being beaten and ridiculed by the soldiers and the mob alike. Golgotha was the final place where Jesus endured tremendous pain and agony. It is also there where we witnessed His great love for humanity. Without complaint, He was nailed to that cross, dying a sinner's death. As Jesus hung on that cross, His mind was on you. God came to earth as one of us. He put on humanity, and the Bible says that Jesus "...was oppressed and treated harshly, yet he never said a word..." just so that you may live a peaceful and joyous life here on earth with Him while awaiting His soon return.

The last spot those pilgrims look at is the tomb where Jesus was placed after He died. Can you guess what these pilgrims find when they go in the tomb? Nothing! The tomb is empty. Jesus rose from the dead. He is alive, and He will soon return the second time to take us home. He will come, not as an infant, but as Lord of lords and King of kings.

You can visit the tomb of Mohammed or Buddha. You can visit the tombs of any religious leader you desire, and you will find their remains. But when you visit the tomb where our Creator was placed, you will find it empty. He says, "I am the resurrection and the life. He who believes in Me, though he may die, he shall live." (John 11:25 NKJ)

A couple of years ago, my father suffered a terrible car accident on the streets of Texas as he was heading to our native country of El Salvador. I will never forget that terrible Saturday night. Before we had any knowledge of the accident, I was feeling eerie and very tired. That night I went to bed early, something I never did when I was in my early twenties. As I was asleep, my brother shook my feet and called my name, asking me to wake up. I kicked my feet at him, wanting him to leave me alone, and then he said something that just got my attention.

He said, "Rene, wake up. Our dad is dead."

I got half way up and said to him, "Listen, brother, if you are joking, I will pounce on you."

"No, it is not a joke. He suffered a car accident. He is dead."

I got up from my bed, wanting to confirm what my brother had told me, I went downstairs to see my mom. She was sitting at the kitchen table with her head on it, her arms around her head. Tears rolled down her cheeks. I did not say a word. What my brother told me was true. Our father was dead.

In shock I headed to my room and threw myself on my knees. I felt a tingling sensation all over my body. I remembered how a few days ago my father had wanted to say goodbye to me and wanted to take me out for lunch. My excuse for not eating with him was, "I have too much work." That was a lie. My parents had split up when I was about thirteen years of age, and my relationship with my dad was not good. I did not want to spend any time with my dad before he traveled to El Salvador.

On my knees, I recalled the day I gave my heart to Jesus. It was an exhilarating moment. I thought my feelings towards my dad were going to change. After all, I was a Christian. Now at the thought of never again having the chance to say hello to my dad, haunted me. Just one more chance, just one more chance to tell him how much I loved him. I cried, "Just one more chance to tell him of You, my Lord."

As I was on my knees, my heart sank. My body quivered as I pleaded with my last ounce of strength. I pleaded to God to give me one more chance.

That night I recall having a high volume of calls from friends and relatives, showing respects for the death of my father. So many people called, and so many relatives came to our apartment. My brother, my mom, and I we were drained. All we wanted was to be left alone while we processed this news by ourselves. That night seemed to be prolonged more than any other night. When you get a blow such as this, the last thing you want is for people to be in your face all night long.

I don't remember at what point of the night we managed to get some sleep. All was a blur. The next day, the phone rang. It was one of my brothers who was with my dad when the accident occurred. He called to let us now that my father was fine. He was not dead. My father began to breathe the night before about the time I was pleading with the God of the impossible.

"Our father is not dead, but alive." came the voice from the phone. When I heard this news, I was elated, and began to jump up and down praising my God for what he had done.

From this experience I got a glimpse of how Mary and the disciples must have felt when they realized that Jesus was not dead but alive.

A while ago, my daughter and I went to Israel, where our Lord had lived and where He walked among men. We saw the Sea of Galilee and imagined the Peter walking on water, doing the impossible. Only when you are with Jesus is the impossible, possible. After traveling all over that marvelous land, we went to relax at the Dead Sea. The next day we were on our way to walk on the Via Dolorosa or "the way of suffering," where it is said that our Lord stumbled His way to Golgotha, also known as "the place of skull". It was on that hill called Golgotha that our Savior was nailed to a cross and was crucified between two criminals. There they divided His garments and casted lots for them. On the top of the cross was placed an inscription stating, "This is Jesus, the King of the Jews." (Matthew 26:37 NKJ)

Our last stop was at the tomb where Joseph of Arimathea had placed the body of Jesus. It was at this tomb that our Lord was laid to rest that Friday evening. Millions of people go to Israel every year, to experience for themselves the grandeur of walking where our Lord walked. Millions of people see what my daughter and I saw, and before their journey in Israel is over, they all head to the tomb. What do you suppose they all see when at the tomb of Jesus? Nothing. Nothing. The tomb is empty. Every tourist gets a look at an empty tomb. I saw it with my own eyes, and I am here to inform you, the tomb is empty. Jesus rose from the dead, just as he promised. Our God is not dead. He is alive. Tell it to everyone you see on the streets. Our God is not dead. He is alive.

This God I serve wants to bring joy into your life, joy into your everyday activities. Our God is alive. Come to Him just as you are, take pleasure in all that God has in store for you. There is nothing impossible for Him. Find out for yourself what He has in store for you. You will never regret it. Our God is the God of the impossible, and He wants to do the impossible in your life. Come to Him. Trust Him, and give your life to this omnipotent, sovereign God. He is, after all, the God of the Impossible.